The Complete Book of
TRADITIONAL
FAIR ISLE KNITTING

A Shetland couple from Gulberwick, in traditional dress (Dennis Coutts)

THE COMPLETE BOOK
OF
TRADITIONAL FAIR ISLE KNITTING

Sheila McGregor

Charles Scribner's Sons, *New York*

Library of Congress Catalog Card Number 81–85781
ISBN 0–684–18707–8

Published simultaneously in Canada by Collier Macmillan Canada, Inc.

Printed in Great Britain

Second Edition

Contents

Acknowledgements

This book has been in preparation for several years and I owe a considerable debt to a great many people, principally to the friendly and skilful knitters of Shetland. Special mention must be made of the Shetland Federation of the Scottish Women's Rural Institutes and its individual members in many parts. I am also most grateful to the staffs of the Shetland Museum, Lerwick, the National Museum of Antiquities of Scotland in Edinburgh (NMAS), the Royal Scottish Museum, also in Edinburgh, the Victoria and Albert Museum in London and the National Library of Scotland, Edinburgh. I have greatly appreciated their consistent and courteous interest and practical help.

Much help has been received from other individuals, in particular from the late Dr George Waterston, Mr K. G. Ponting, Dr Michael Ryder, Mr Walter Scott, Mr John Johnston, Mr Gilbert Johnston and Mr Michael Peterson. Invaluable assistance has been given by Mr Pieter Hintjens, without whose labours in the darkroom this book would not have been possible, and other photographers and friends. Those illustrations not credited are from the author's collection.

Although in some cases the knitters of garments used in illustrations are known to me, it has been impossible to trace all of them. It was therefore decided that individual acknowledgement of knitters would be inappropriate. To all of these highly skilled and original craftswomen goes this common acknowledgement of their essential contribution to this record of their achievement.

Introduction

Hand knitting, once a major British industry, has regained much of its former respectability since the days, not long ago, when it was described as a suitable occupation only for the aged and feeble-minded.

In one part of Britain, the Shetland Islands, a group of islands off the north-east tip of Scotland beyond the Orkneys, hand knitting has persisted as a cottage industry over almost 500 years. Various factors now threaten this old heritage, particularly North Sea oil and the prosperity brought by the influx of oil-related jobs. In many communities (though not in all) the most expert knitters are increasingly the elderly ones, and there is some danger that old skills and old patterns may be lost. Now seems therefore an appropriate point to make a comprehensive record of the craft of stranded knitting in Shetland.

To most people this is more familiar as Fair Isle knitting, and indeed it was in Fair Isle, an outlying island of the Shetland group, that this brightly coloured and patterned stranded knitting was first developed. It uses two colours in each row and the wool not in use is stranded along the back in short loops. This forms a double fabric which is extremely warm and resistant to all but the worst weather.

It is possible, but not very relevant, to distinguish between the Fair Isle knitting of Fair Isle and the Fair Isle knitting of the rest of Shetland. The purely 'Fair Isle' period lasted from about 1850 to 1910 or so; thereafter most other parts of Shetland began to produce very similar stranded knitting, using the old patterns of Fair Isle, possibly some small local ones from other islands, and adding a great many from other sources. Today most knitting in Shetland is of 'Fair Isle' type – stranded knitting using the traditional patterns which have been collected here. Fair Isle itself, sadly, is no longer a very active centre, but the fishing islands of Whalsay, Burra and the Out Skerries, together with Lerwick on the largest island, Mainland, have thriving and innovative communities of knitters.

Both techniques and patterns have been recorded here. The unusual knitting method used in Shetland is mentioned but not stressed. It is quite possible to knit these patterns with any technique, so long as the circular method is followed. (This is described in Chapter 4: Knitting Techniques.)

The Pattern Notebook in Part Three contains the many patterns familiar to Shetland knitters, arranged according to size. My apologies are extended for any favourites inadvertently omitted. These patterns are all regarded by the Shetlanders as traditional.

The main source has been present-day knitters and knitwear but old patterns from museum pieces have been recorded as well. Besides their great interest to hand knitters, these patterns will be found useful by other craft workers and are adaptable to many types of embroidery as well as to machine knitting.

The origins of this amazing collection of patterns have aroused much speculation and some controversy. The writer has spent considerable time over the past few years investigating the popular theories and believes that while her account is not complete it is based on fact rather than romantic fiction. The remarkable achievements of the hand knitters of nineteenth-century Fair Isle, who produced brilliant and exciting knitting in surroundings of extreme poverty and hardship, deserve more credit than is generally given.

PART ONE

BACKGROUND AND ORIGINS

Traditional fisherman's cap from Yell, Shetland

1 The Background to the Fair Isle Patterns

The Shetland Islands lie far north of the Scottish mainland, so far north that on most maps they occupy a small box in an otherwise empty corner. Air travel has made communications much easier in recent years but in earlier times, when sea travel was safer and quicker than any other method, their isolation was less marked compared with many other places. Indeed, in a seagoing context, many routes converge on Shetland, from the Baltic, Scandinavia, and the North Sea. The Faeroe Islands are a short sail north again, as is Iceland. The Shetland Islands have always been easy to get to from the south, by way of Orkney and Fair Isle from mainland Scotland or the Hebrides. This is how most settlers have reached them, from the earliest pioneers some 5,000 years ago, who settled there with their sheep and cattle.

They were followed by other immigrants from the south during the Celtic period which lasted until the coming of the Vikings in about AD 700. From 876 to 1379 Shetland was administered from Norway, though from about 1200 onwards the link became increasingly tenuous and Scottish influence replaced that of Norway. In 1468 a transaction took place which has caused great indignation among Norse-minded people ever since – the mortgaging of Orkney and Shetland to provide the balance of the dowry of Margaret of Denmark on her marriage to King James III of Scotland. In fact this recognised the fact that by then the islands were far more Scottish than Norwegian.

The following period was not altogether a happy one, with the introduction of the feudal system under the Stewart Earls and consequent exploitation. Mainland Scotland is still regarded as a foreign place by Shetlanders, a source of 'dear meal and bad ministers'. Nevertheless, a visitor to Shetland from Scotland will not find the islands foreign. The scenery is hilly, with rough pasture almost to sea level; the sea is never far away and the dialect, at least on the largest island, Mainland, sounds reassuringly Scottish.

Shetland today presents great contrasts. Lerwick, the capital, main port and only town of any size, is a busy centre of oil-related service industries. Its harbour has tripled in size, and oil rigs are regularly parked in the bay south of the town. And yet the crofter in the next township, out to feed his hens or move the tethered lamb to a new spot, will barely give them a glance. Shetland has seen many previous surges of activity and survived both the attendant prosperity and the inevitable depressions which have followed.

Fair Isle lies to the south of Shetland, midway between the southern tip of Mainland and Orkney. It has always been regarded as part of Shetland, geographically and culturally. Its two main claims to fame are the shipwreck on the island of the Armada flagship, *El Gran Griffon*, and the brightly patterned knitwear that has become familiar all over the world. Like Shetland, Fair Isle was relatively less isolated in days of sail and indeed lay across a busy sea route to North America. The island also acts as a convenient landfall for small boats sailing between Orkney and Shetland, the high cliffs at the north end being visible from a great distance at sea.

Knitting probably reached Shetland from mainland Scotland around AD 1500. Its immediate popularity and lasting importance in those northerly islands have much to do with the Shetland climate and the excellent fine wool produced by the native breed of sheep. While Shetland seldom experiences much snow or frost, it has more than its share of gales, fog and general pervading dampness. Few garments are better suited to resist this type of weather than those knitted of Shetland wool.

In common with most other-parts of Scotland where there was a supply of suitable wool, hand knitting rapidly developed into a major cottage industry in the sixteenth and later centuries. The main articles produced for trade were coarse stockings in enormous numbers, together with such other small items as nightcaps, waistcoats (i.e. knitted underwear) and gloves.

This hosiery trade flourished throughout Scotland until Victorian times, when it dwindled and died in most places as machine-knitted stockings replaced the hand-knitted ones. Shetland is unique in still having a hand knitting industry. The patterns which form the subject of this book have played no small part in the survival of this cottage industry. With an entrepreneur in virtually every second cottage it has always been difficult to estimate its importance, but proceeds from hand knitting, while not reflecting either the time or the craftsmanship involved, still make a useful contribution to many island budgets.

The bright and unusual patterns worked into the traditional knitting of Fair Isle first attracted

Ferrying sheep (NMAS)

Fisherman's cap with Fair-Isle-type patterns; nineteenth century

attention in 1856, when they were described by Miss Eliza Edmondston, a member of a distinguished Shetland family, in her book *Sketches and Tales of the Shetland Islands*. She follows an excellent and obviously first-hand description of their complexity and layout with a purely speculative and quite unsupported suggestion that there was a connection between these extraordinary patterns and the wrecking on the island in 1588 of the Spanish Armada flagship *El Gran Griffon*, mentioned previously. This romantic myth achieved instant success, which it still enjoys in many quarters, despite its total improbability. More modern theories tend to favour a Scandinavian influence. There appears to be equally little truth in this and the subject of the origin of these patterns will be dealt with in detail in the next chapter.

These 'outlandish' patterns had limited appeal to Victorians, though Fair Isle knitwear did travel to the Antarctic with the *Scotia* expedition of 1902,

which was financed by the Paisley firm of J. & P. Coats Limited. James Coats was a regular visitor to Fair Isle and took a paternalistic interest in the well-being of the islanders. At this time Mainland Shetland was still engrossed in the knitting of lace shawls and veils, though this was a declining trade, and smaller articles such as gloves and underwear. There was some tradition of stranded knitting in two colours, but it was restricted to small pattern bands on stockings, purses and gloves and the traditional fishermen's bag-caps or stocking caps, striped, it was said, like signal flags.

Stranded knitting became increasingly popular all over Shetland after about 1910. The old patterns of Fair Isle were copied, among many others, and memories are still alive of these patterns being passed from croft to croft on scraps of paper. In many places there seems to have been little idea of how best to apply them to actual garments and some unusual designs have resulted. One such

An early mainland scarf in moorit, orange and green

unusual scarf is illustrated. It is knitted mainly in the fine, soft 'moorit' (russet) wool preferred by Mainland knitters for scarves, but instead of being in openwork, as normal, it is in plain knitting with decorated ends. The patterns are those of Fair Isle but the colours, two shades of green and one of orange, are not. They were probably home-dyed with Fairy Dyes or shop-bought to conform to some verbal instruction about the need to use bright colours.

Throughout the 1920s, Mainland knitters and Fair Isle knitters continued to experiment with patterns and colour. A great many new patterns were added to the repertoire at about this time. In general it was a period of great innovation in knitting. One major innovation was the adoption and adaptation of the fisherman's working garment, the jersey or gansie (Guernsey), as leisure wear for all classes. It is difficult today to imagine life without the comfort and convenience of jerseys, cardigans and all the other knitwear we take for granted, but they are a very modern fashion. The knitters of Shetland were not slow to take it up

and began to knit 'allover' jerseys and pullovers. The very earliest, from Fair Isle, date from about 1910. They are fragile things, knitted with home-spun, home-dyed wool in indigo blue, madder red, gold and natural white. Commercial jersey knitting had to wait for the availability of more suitable yarn, machine-spun and mill-dyed, both to save time which could more profitably be spent knitting than spinning, and to provide the necessary quantities of thicker yarn of uniform quality and colour.

This new fashion gained the Royal seal of approval in 1921 when the Prince of Wales wore a jersey presented by a firm of Lerwick drapers to play golf at St Andrews.

Today hand knitting is still important in Shetland, both as a cottage industry and as a craft. The former is declining in the face of machine knitting and oil-related employment, but the gansie knitting of the fishing communities is still very active, both to provide working gansies for the menfolk and to fill orders from Mainland Shetland and the south.

Golfer in Fair Isle pullover similar to that presented to HRH the Prince of Wales in 1921 by the firm that also produced this one (James A. Smith, Drapers, Lerwick)

The Origins of the Patterns

It is easy to jump to conclusions when looking for the origins of the numerous and varied patterns used in Shetland knitting today. For one thing, many knitted patterns from very different traditions in different countries have much in common. To a large extent, this is a result of the technique which they share – certain patterns are by definition easier to knit and will therefore be more popular wherever stranded knitting is done.

To trace direct influence it is important to be quite familiar with the Shetland patterns. They have several common features. Most are fairly small and simple, as textile patterns go. Almost all are symmetrical; indeed most are very strongly symmetrical, with eight similar parts. As a result, most are geometric rather than representational. There is a preference for diagonal lines over strong vertical lines, and by far the larger number have an odd number of rows. The reasons for this are basic to the craft of knitting, particularly when patterns are not printed and are copied from small samples or knitted from memory.

Unlike embroidery workers, knitters do not have the benefit of a marked canvas on which they can count threads and place stitches. They are creating their own fabric as they work along the rows, knitting into space. Symmetrical patterns make this easier. Once a pattern has been 'set', each row grows in regular fashion from the preceding, and the second half of every pattern can be copied from the first. Most Shetland patterns can be knitted vertically or across with identical results. Strong vertical lines tend to be avoided as they can easily pull together and tighten at the back of the work. Diagonal lines make for more elastic knitting.

Most patterns avoid long stretches in one colour. This again depends on the technique of stranded knitting. Both colours of wool must be kept moving to avoid long loops on the reverse of the work.

Any experimentation with patterns of this kind will quickly show why they tend to have an odd number of rows. From the design point of view, those with an even number are almost always more clumsy and less symmetrical. Moreover, Shetland knitters like to have a centre row and often knit it in bright colours for emphasis.

One last feature, less easy to define but easy enough to recognise, distinguishes patterns popular in Shetland with those of many neighbouring countries such as Norway. It is the liking for little motifs and for a pattern to be 'finished'. Lines, in Shetland patterns, usually link up in a satisfying space-enclosing way with other lines, and the spaces so enclosed are usually decorated with one or several of the little motifs in the Shetland repertoire. Repeated diagonals, probably copied from weaving and popular in Norwegian knitting traditions, have been edited out in favour of more concrete designs.

The liking for symmetrical, geometric, diagonal shapes is shared with many other textile techniques such as kelim and twill weaving, several simple types of embroidery and lacework, and so on. There is a shared need to keep threads moving diagonally and to memorise patterns. One result of this is that some patterns have a very wide distribution indeed. For example, one of the large stars is embroidered in Greece, worked in beads by Plains Indians and in barkcloth in Fiji. It is familiar in the Thai Highlands, and in Norway, where it is as likely to be embroidered as knitted. In Shetland it would certainly be knitted and probably thought of as a Norwegian snowflake.

In the Pattern Notebook the patterns used today in stranded knitting in Shetland have been arranged according to size. This divides them usefully into groups of broadly similar origins.

Firstly there are the Peerie Patterns, 'peerie' being the Shetland vernacular for 'small'. Most occupy 5 or 7 rows and are knitted in horizontal bands as part of a more complex pattern. Many are also used in vertical arrangements.

Patterns filling 9 to 13 rows can best be described as Border Patterns, though they also are knitted in bands, alternating with larger or smaller patterns as part of a complex repeat. Many have larger and smaller versions.

Traditional Fair Isle patterns from the old pieces known to have been knitted on that island generally fill 15 or 17 rows in the original versions. They consist of six- or eight-sided lozenges containing a motif or some other decoration and linked along the row by elaborate crosses. These are the so-called *OXO* patterns. The crosses must be understood as joining devices rather than as separate decorative elements.

Then there are the Large Stars. Most take up 21, 25 or 31 rows. While much larger versions exist and can certainly be knitted, they are less flexible in an allover design and become difficult to memorise or copy easily.

Old cap knitted in silk, showing very early use of the Fair Isle OXO pattern

Lastly, there are allover patterns in great variety. Most are decorated diagonal frameworks or variations on the star-and-diamond theme. There are also many diced patterns and a few older patterns made up of small crosses repeated in rows.

It will probably surprise many readers to learn that these patterns were not used in Shetland before the early years of this century, although many have longer histories in other places. The exceptions are the large and elaborate *OXO* patterns of Fair Isle described above, and certain of the peerie patterns (shown here) which were used together with the *OXO* patterns in early pieces from Fair Isle. Similar small patterns are found in other places around the North Sea and may well have been knitted for hundreds of years. There is little evidence for this apart from some very small patterns on old socks and a purse in the Shetland Museum, and nineteenth century descriptions of patterns on fishermen's traditional caps.

The origin of the large *OXO* patterns has

aroused much speculation, as has already been mentioned. An early suggestion already mentioned linked them to the Spanish soldiers shipwrecked on Fair Isle almost 300 years before the patterns were first recorded. There is however little in common between Spanish textile patterns of the time and the Fair Isle patterns. Moreover, a look at any early account of the well-documented shipwreck of *El Gran Griffon* on Fair Isle in late September 1588 will make the tale of comfortable collaboration seem very unlikely. It is possible that some of the more extreme details were added by later writers, but the tale is not one that needs much added colour. For six weeks, from September to November, almost 300 men were stranded on a very small island which at that time supported only 50 people (17 families). Many of the Spaniards died of starvation. Several are said to have been thrown over the cliffs by the islanders, themselves faced with starvation in the face of winter. Not until 1856 was any connection suggested between this

Old allover patterns. These have much in common with Faeroese and Baltic patterns

Peerie patterns; a selection of the oldest, used in Fair Isle before 1900

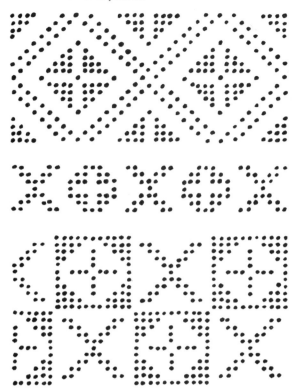

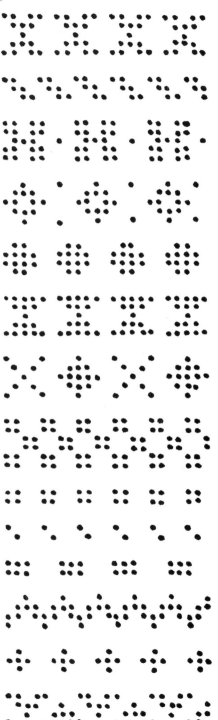

remote and unhappy episode and the colourful and unusual patterns then being knitted on the island.

In spite of the total lack of evidence or even historical probability, this romantic fiction was immediately popular with the Victorian public. As early as 1870 the islanders were denying vigorously, if vainly, that they had learned anything about knitting from the Spaniards, 'though it had become the fashion to say so'.

Their own memory of the arrival of the patterns on Fair Isle is more pedestrian but more likely to be true. Folk memory on Fair Isle, as in other such places, is tenacious and accurate. Their story is that a sailor, a Fair Isle man, brought home a shawl which had patterns which the Fair Isle women tried to knit, with considerable success. From then on they are said to have continued to knit the same patterns, adding others and adapting them 'to almost the present day' (which in this story was 1945). This story is well supported by

Early Fair Isle patterns showing the influence of woven originals

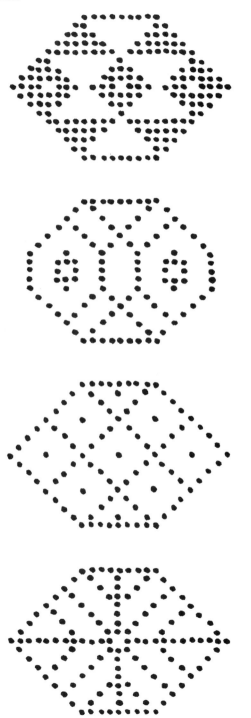

the internal evidence of the oldest known pattern layout, which appears to reflect a woven original. It also rings very true to anyone who knows modern Shetland knitters and their strong aversion to repeating a design. It is unlikely, to say the least, that any Shetlander (which by definition includes any Fair Islander) would be content to knit the same pattern in the same layout over hundreds of years. Even the earliest and most formal Fair Isle pieces show a continuous process of change. New ideas (for example, introducing the older Peerie Patterns) and new arrangements of existing elements are devised for every new garment knitted, as indeed they still are today.

The date of this development in stranded knitting, which has led to what has been called Fair Isle knitting of one kind or another becoming familiar to people all over the world, was probably around 1850. There are several reasons for suggesting such a date. Earlier visitors to Fair Isle (it was surprisingly well visited in the nineteenth century) seldom mention knitting except as a routine export in the form of coarse hose. Sir Walter Scott was a reliable and observant witness who visited the island in 1814 and noted only the fishermen's caps already referred to. Not until 1856 was mention made of large, bright patterns and thereafter most visitors record them in recognisable detail.

A date of around 1850 also fits in with the known history of dyeing in Shetland. The earliest Fair Isle knitting which survives invariably uses wool dyed with imported madder and indigo (natural dark brown is occasionally used as a substitute for indigo). Many local vegetable dyes are available on Fair Isle and could have been used. The fact that imported dyes were used instead, in colour combinations which remained unchanged throughout the known history of Fair Isle knitting, suggests strongly that the patterns were first knitted after the introduction of imported vegetable dyes. Neither the rich red of madder nor the splendid blue of indigo could be matched by any local dyes, nor is there much evidence of experiment with colour other than the substitution of naturally-coloured dark brown wool for indigo, mentioned above. The patterns used varied considerably, but the same colour sequence was used for all of them; bands of red with white and dark blue (or dark brown) with gold alternate in every old piece. The gold dye could be got from a number of local plants, such as ragwort and bistort.

Fair Isle socks

Now the first mentioned of imported dyes in Shetland is in 1840 and it would be reasonable to expect the people of Fair Isle to learn about them shortly after that. Certainly these bright and pleasing colours have been chosen from the first as though to match some existing convention. If you like the story of the shawl mentioned earlier – that present from abroad which so influenced Fair Isle knitting – the bright red and blue dyes would be chosen to match the colours woven into it, which is what the Fair Isle people themselves claimed.

It would be nice to be able to say at this point that the shawl came from Norway, or Aberdeen, or somewhere specific. That would neatly tie up the origin of the oldest and most unusual Fair Isle patterns. First, however, one needs to ask: Where might a Fair Isle man have gone shopping for a present for home? The answer, of course, is almost anywhere in the world – Shetlanders are still great travellers by sea and, for the Fair Isle men of the nineteenth century, working as crew on a merchant ship was one of the few possible ways of earning a living. With such a vast area to search, it is perhaps not surprising that so far no exact original has been found.

There is, however, some circumstantial evidence to suggest that the most likely source is in the Baltic. Today such countries as Estonia and Lithuania seem remote, but in the days of sailing ships there were close links between the Baltic and Shetland. Lerwick is a useful port of call for ships sailing to North America from the Baltic, and much timber was imported from the Baltic to treeless Shetland. While no exactly similar patterns have been found, the folk weaving of the Baltic area and Russia has many patterns of the right complexity.

Of equal interest is the fact that stranded knitting in bright colours was well developed in the Baltic states long before it reached its heyday in Shetland. It may well have predated the Fair Isle innovation as well. Intricate allover jerseys were knitted in Estonia, with patterns very similar to those developed in recent years in Whalsay.

Mitten, glove and stocking patterns exist in huge numbers, which indicates a long-standing tradition. Estonia, for example, has hundreds of mitten patterns, compared with a few dozen in nearby Finland and a small handful in distant Shetland and Norway. Estonia also has an interesting tradition of plain knitted gloves and stockings decorated with embroidered patterns. This firmly links traditional embroidery patterns with later knitted patterns, including some still used on glove fingers in Shetland today.

Such patterns could have arrived in Shetland from the Baltic both by diffusion overland through Finland and Norway (the old glove and mitten patterns probably went this way), and by direct imports into Shetland of patterned Baltic knitwear. It would be satisfying to find evidence of any such direct link and, by happy coincidence, a cap in the collection of the Shetland Museum provides just such a link. Although described as a fisherman's cap from Yell (a northerly island in the Shetland group), its pattern is totally unlike any other recorded from any period in Shetland

Pattern from an Estonian jersey; nineteenth century

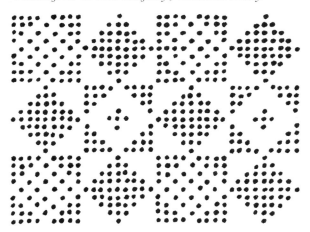

Close-up of a multi-coloured fisherman's cap in the collection of the Shetland Museum

knitting. It would, however, be perfectly at home in Estonia and either the cap or the pattern must have been imported from there.

A Scandinavian origin for the patterns (both the Fair Isle *OXO* patterns and the collection *in toto*) is often proffered as an alternative to the Spanish connection but, with the exception of the Large Stars, there is no evidence for any direct influence on Shetland knitting from Norway or, for that matter, anywhere else in Scandinavia. The large *OXO* patterns are very much more complex than any found in Norwegian folk textiles, whether knitted or woven. It does indeed seem that Shetland has provided inspiration and stimulus to the knitting traditions of Scandinavia rather than the other way round. For example, the large, more complex and more colourful patterns knitted today in Faeroe are known locally as 'Shetland' patterns.

The main contribution of Norwegian design has been the Large Stars. Those used in Norwegian knitting are on the whole small and plain and the larger and more decorated versions popular in Shetland are probably from embroidered rather than knitted originals. Wherever they have been collected from, the Large Stars became popular during World War II, when there was a considerable influx of Norwegian refugees into Shetland. They are used in many ways today in Shetland, and feature particularly in the allover gansie designs of the fishing communities such as Whalsay. These star-and-diamond patterns are very like others involving eight-pointed stars, such as are found, for example, in Russian folk lacework. But the designs of Whalsay are entirely their own, and

the similarity is a coincidence.

What of the hundreds of other peerie patterns and border patterns found today in Shetland knitting? These were in fact all well known throughout the nineteenth century and in earlier times, though generally as embroidered patterns rather than knitted ones. The most striking collection of similar patterns is found in the finely worked cross-stitch samplers made in the second half of the nineteenth century in the Muller Homes in Bristol and often known as Bristol Orphanage samplers. One such sampler contains 78 different border patterns as well as a number of single motifs such as hearts, anchors, crosses and stars.

Most of these border patterns could be knitted as embroidered in cross-stitch, and an extraordinarily high proportion are known to Shetland knitters today, some with minor adaptations to make them easier to knit. The orphans knew the 'blocks', several versions of the key pattern, and a great many zig-zag and diamond variations. Many of the frames, later used in Shetland allover pat-

Norwegian Jersey patterns

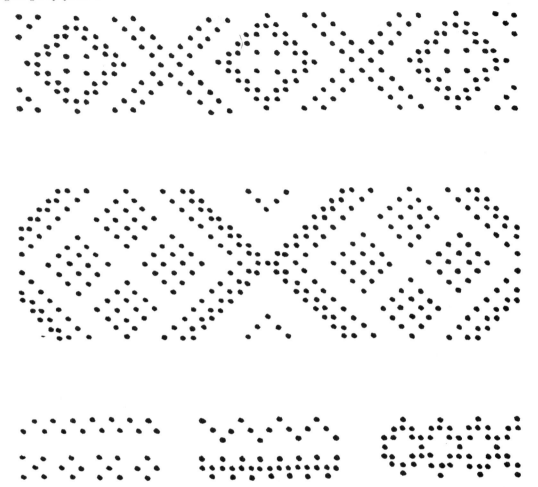

terns, appear here – the feathers, the wreath, the little blocks of four. The samplers also contain many devices more familiar to us from Oriental carpets.

Such patterns were published in little booklets sold by Victorian drapers. These had a selection of standard alphabets, numerals and borders (intended for marking linen) printed on one side and were published all over Europe. Those from Germany have most in common with the type of pattern now used in Shetland.

It is impossible at this distance to find exactly how they came to Shetland. Perhaps they were collected by individuals from old embroidery booklets and copied by one knitter from another. Perhaps these old booklets, or the samplers, were

used as source material for the sheets of stencilled patterns sold as knitting patterns in Lerwick in 1920. These achieved great popularity, and carefully preserved sheets are still in use.

These cross-stitch patterns were copied from older patterns with a very long history indeed. The ancient lacework technique known as cut-and-drawn work (known all over Europe under a variety of names) used many geometric patterns – crosses, diamonds, stars, hearts, angular flowers – which are very suitable both for cross-stitch and for stranded knitting.

An Oriental influence has often been detected in Shetland knitting patterns. Popular explanations for this sometimes go as far back as the Vikings. Links with the East did not, however, start with

Faeroese allover patterns (seeding) and border patterns

Allover lace pattern from a nineteenth-century Russian pattern book

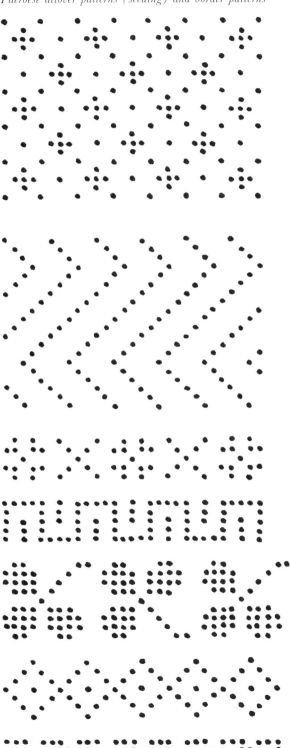

the Vikings, nor were they the last people to venture down the East River Route to the Caspian and the treasures (in a design sense) of the Caucasus. Designers still make this journey frequently, though now they seldom travel further than the nearest well-stocked library. It may, once again, be less romantic, but it is certainly true that many Oriental patterns knitted in Shetland today were copied from lace curtains and linoleum.

Scotland has made a modest contribution in the form of the diced patterns, originally knitted as kilt hose and then popular for knickerbocker hose. Shetland knitters like to decorate these diced patterns. Other influences have almost certainly included Sanquhar gloves, Scottish Fleet gansies and modern commercial knitting leaflets.

Bristol Orphanage samplers; a small selection of the many border patterns which have much in common with twentieth-century Shetland knitting patterns

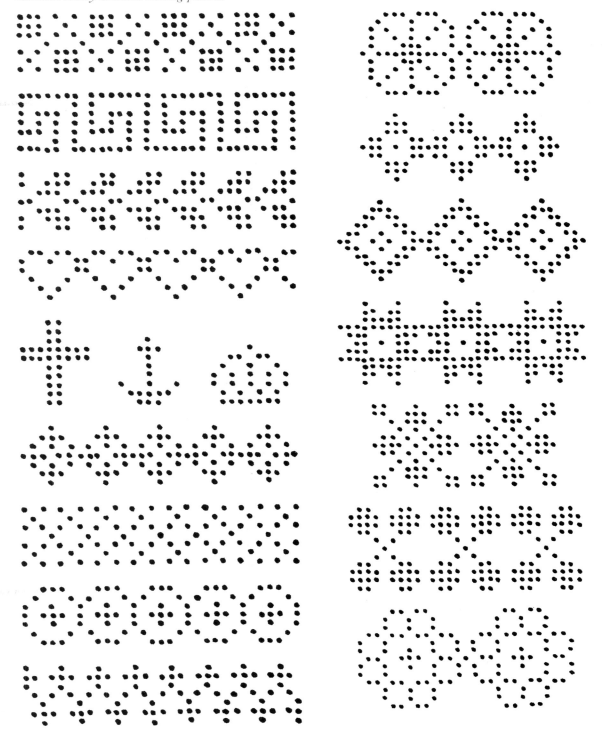

Nineteenth-century German cross-stitch patterns (left)
compared with twentieth-century Shetland knitting patterns
(right)   *The linoleum star*

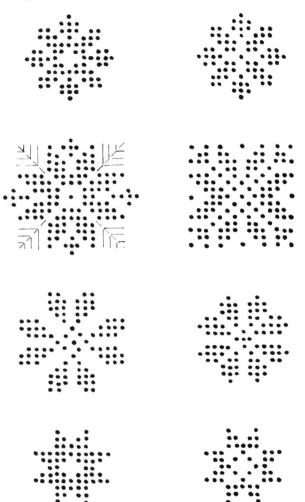

PART TWO

DESIGN, TECHNIQUES AND COLOUR

A ski cap with border pattern and fancy crown

3 Designing a Fair Isle Garment

This chapter covers the general principles of applying Fair Isle patterns to any garment, with a few examples and descriptions of typical Shetland layouts. Design methods for different garments are then described in more detail, but it must be emphasised that it would be out of place and indeed misleading to give stitch-by-stitch instructions. Any detailed descriptions are intended only as helpful guidelines. However, anyone wishing to learn Fair Isle knitting and equipped with the choice of patterns at the end of this book will find it easy, and great fun, to design their own knitwear, and will have all the more pleasure from knowing that it is unique, as all true Fair Isle knitting is.

Detailed practical knitting techniques are described in Chapter 4. To avoid duplication, reference will be made to relevant sections in Chapter 4 using bold type (e.g. **Casting On**). The most important headings in Chapter 4 (which is in alphabetic order) are **Circular Knitting, Stranded Knitting,** and **Tension.** The use of colour is discussed in Chapter 5.

General rules in planning a Fair Isle garment

Fair Isle knitting is circular, stranded knitting, with the patterns knitted in by the use of two contrasting colours in each row. Apart from any ribbing, purl stitches are not used. Shetlanders have continued to use the elegant and easy seamless method of knitting even for unpatterned work long after it has been replaced on mainland Britain by flat knitting, probably as a result of overdependence on simplified commercial knitting leaflets. Knitting in the round was the only method known in Britain for jersey knitting until the 1930s and is still used for traditional gansies and in Scandinavian countries.

Circular knitting makes working with two wools a relatively easy matter. Bulky seams are further avoided by **grafting,** putting stitches aside on a stitch holder or **picking up stitches.** The time spent learning such techniques as grafting is more than saved later, and the absence of seams makes for a comfortable and professional finish.

The steps in designing a Fair Isle garment are simple to grasp and fun to work out. There are four main steps: tension, size, number of stitches and pattern choice.

1 Work out your **tension** (and try out a colour scheme at the same time) by knitting a Fair Isle sample, either a flat piece with the wools broken off and joined in again at every row, or a small tube of about a hand's width. Use the size of needles planned, and the yarns to be used. Commercial patterns can be useful here, to give an indication of suitable needle size and tension for a particular yarn. If slightly firmer work is desired, use a needle one size smaller, and knit another sample. A needle one size larger will give slightly looser work.

2 Establish the size of the garment to be knitted by measuring an existing one, or by reference to a good commercial pattern. To fit a known chest measurement, a jersey should be approximately 5cm (2in) larger than the body measurement.

3 Work out the number of stitches needed by multiplying the size (chest measurement, circumference of a ski cap, etc.) by the tension, e.g., a tension of 8 stitches to 2½cm (1in) over a jersey of 100cm (40in) would give 320 stitches. Do the same for the number of rows, measured from above the rib, e.g. a tension of 10 rows to 2½cm (1in) would require 240 rows for 60cm (24in) length. The number of stitches and rows can be adapted slightly, by adding on or taking off 3 or 4 at the most (1cm or ½in) in Jumper Yarn.

It should be noted that the welt (the ribbed lower edge) is usually tighter than the body of a garment, and is cast on with fewer stitches than required for the patterned body (approximately 10 per cent less). It is safer to be too large than too small, though a garment that is slightly too small can be stretched a little by careful dressing. Shrinking to fit is not recommended.

4 Choose or adapt patterns from the Pattern Notebook to fit the stitches and rows.

The choice of patterns

In the most expertly designed modern Shetland knitting, patterns are fitted in to make a complete sequence not only horizontally but also vertically, matching perfectly over the shoulder. This involves considerable calculation before a stitch is cast on. However, this is often not possible – indeed, in the earlier days of Fair Isle knitting both on Shetland and on Fair Isle itself, such perfection was seldom achieved. It is no shame to have incomplete patterns but these should be where they will be least conspicuous, e.g. underarm.

The variety of patterns given in the Notebook makes it easier to find the right one for a perfect fit. They have been arranged according to the number of rows they fill, as this figure does not change. Horizontal size has not been indicated for the good reason that the different parts of most border patterns are interchangeable, and they can be fitted together to give widely differing repeats along the row. Any such rearrangement is acceptable, providing the result is 'knittable' and does not have a stretch at any point, along any row, of more than 7 stitches or so.

A great variety of joining devices exists to prevent this happening (see Chapter 6, page 68).

A Ski Cap with Fair Isle Border

One of the simplest things to design and knit is a ski cap. It can be knitted like an unshaped tube, ribbed and turned up at the lower end and gathered to be finished off with a tassel at the top. The cap illustrated has a shaped and decorated crown. This is traditional in Shetland but is not at all essential. If we work though the steps in choosing a pattern for our cap, we will have covered all the processes involved in designing Fair Isle knitting, but on a small and easy scale.

An adult cap might need to be 60cm (24in) for a comfortable fit round the ears. At a possible tension of 8 stitches to 2½cm (1in), we would need 192 stitches over the patterned border. This could be adapted to 190–195 if necessary. The edge would usually be knitted in rib, using fewer stitches, say 175, for a snug fit.

The border can be any chosen depth. Stranded knitting does add thickness and warmth, as well as decoration, and a band wide enough to cover the ears will be practical as well as pretty. Suppose that we choose an 11-row border, framed with two 2-row patterns – this could be indicated as 2/11/2. Shetland knitters usually leave one or more plain, unpatterned rows between patterns (anything from 0 to 5 is common). If we leave the normal 1 row, we then have a pattern band which is 17 rows deep.

We could, just as easily, choose a much deeper border or series of borders: 3/15/3 or 5/11/5 – almost any combination is possible.

The depth of pattern in a ski cap will largely depend on the amount of work which the knitter wishes to put into it. It could, for example, be patterned all over, with a small sequence such as 2/5/2/5 etc., leaving 1 or 2 plain rows between each pattern. Each 2-row pattern and each 5-row pattern might be identical, or you might wish to vary the 5-row pattern at each repeat, or vary both.

Another possibility (and there are many more) is to decorate the lower edge with large stars and the rest with seeding.

Whatever is chosen must fit into the round of 190–195 stitches (or will look much better if it does). A pattern that repeats over 10 stitches will fit in 19 times. A 12-stitch pattern will fit in 16 times (to give 192 stitches). Conversely, a 16-stitch pattern will fit in 12 times. A 15-stitch pattern could be repeated 13 times to give 195 stitches, and a 14-stitch repeat would fit in 14 times to give 196 stitches. With a little arithmetic a great many fits can usually be found.

To find the repeat of any chosen pattern from the chart, count along the row from any stitch through one whole repeat to the stitch before the one first counted – be careful not to count the same stitch twice. Most patterns have repeats in even numbers of stitches.

At a tension of 10 rows to 2½cm (1in) you would need to plan 80 rows to give a length of 20cm (8in). Not all of this need be patterned; indeed, the thickness of stranded knitting would make it difficult to gather the knitting to form the crown and the last third or so should be left plain.

The border patterns, large stars and allover patterns are used in exactly the same way to decorate all other knitted items, from egg cosies to working gansies.

Practical guidelines

Gansies and Jerseys

Gansies, lumber jackets, pullovers, tunics and other knitted tops all use similar knitting techniques, in particular **Circular Knitting, Grafting, Picking up Stitches** and **Stranded Knitting.** The gansie method is important and is described here in some detail.

The Gansie Method

Calculate, as shown earlier in this chapter, the number of stitches needed to fit comfortably round the chest and the number of rows which will give the right length. Plan a pattern to fill the appropriate number of stitches and rows.

Reduce the number of stitches slightly (say, by 1 in 10), cast on all the stitches on a set of long double-ended needles, or one circular needle, and work the rib. **Corrugated ribbing** is recommended and a machine-knitted rib is not. At the top of the rib, change to plain knitting and increase to the complete number of stitches. Set the pattern as planned and check that this has been done correctly. This is most important. The beginning of the round, where the colours and pattern change, may be marked with a strand of a different colour, and should be placed at one side of the jersey.

Traditional gansies have a gusset under the arm, and early Fair Isle gansies copy this feature, which is usually knitted with a dropped shoulder. The gusset is begun some 30–33cm (12–13in) from the beginning by making stitches under the arms, so that, by the time the armhole is reached, and the work measures some 48–50cm (19–20in), there are 25 stitches in it. **To make a gusset,** increase 1 stitch on each side of the centre underarm stitch; knit 3 rounds; increase again, this time leaving 3 stitches between increases; knit 3 rounds; increase again, leaving 5 stitches between increases, and so on, until the armhole is reached (see **increasing**). Traditionally there were no reductions around the armhole, the gusset stitches being left on a stitch-holder, and the sleeve opening bridged by a **steek** of 6–8 stitches cast on for that purpose above the gusset. This allows circular knitting to continue up to shoulder level. The dropped shoulder-line which results if there are no reductions made around the armhole is traditional. Most jerseys today do however have a **fitted or semi-fitted shoulder line,** and no gusset. Best results are got by reducing 5–10cm (2–4in) underarm. At least half the stitches are put on a stitch-holder in the first row and the remainder reduced as quickly as possible in following rows. If overdone, this shaping results in the sleeve lying out of line, above the shoulder line. A steek is knitted as above.

The shoulder is joined by **grafting** or **casting-off together.** The top of the steek may be cast off separately, and the armhole opened by cutting it up the centre.

The stitches for the sleeves are then picked up by knitting into the edge of the steek round the armhole and adding on those left, when reducing or from the gusset, on holders. The sleeve is knitted in the round down to the cuff, reducing the

A 1975 Shetland Trader *design, child's size. Note the corrugated rib*

gusset (if knitted) every 3 rows, and decreasing steadily almost to the wrist. If a circular needle has been used, it must be replaced by a set of four for the sleeve. The cuff is traditionally knitted in 2&2 rib.

The top pattern in a sleeve is the one used on the body just above the armhole. The sleeve patterns are knitted down usually in reverse order, and patterns should appear more or less continuous across jersey and sleeves in wear.

The neck can be shaped or unshaped, according to taste, and traditionally was not, being knitted straight up from stitches left on holders, in 1&1 rib, and fastened at the side with buttons.

'The traditional shape is more or less square and offers great scope for decoration.' The sleeves are knitted short to keep them dry and clean. Separate knitted cuffs are worn over them at sea

Choice of Wool

To a large extent, development of jersey knitting, from the early days of heavy, navy gansies to the present great production of Fair Isle patterned jerseys of all kinds, has depended on the wool available. Hand-spun wool was seldom thick enough or strong enough, and mill-spun wool, for all that its critics say, is reliable in colour and weight or, at least, reliable enough to compensate for the lack of control of the process. Today it is mainly mill-spun 2-ply and 3-ply Shetland jumper yarn that is used in Shetland for jerseys and other garments.

Working gansies are more often knitted in chunky synthetic yarn. This is thick, warm, and easy to wash and tumble-dry, an important consideration for a fisherman's wife, especially when she is also the knitter. Colours in synthetic yarns are more limited but practical.

Choice of Patterns

A Fair Isle patterned gansie is virtually double fabric and therefore warm. It is a comfortable, loose shape and thus suitable for a working or leisure jersey. The traditional shape is more or less square and offers great scope for decoration.

Border patterns

Most jerseys are decorated with a variety of border patterns. Shetlanders have collected these for generations and refined their use to a degree not far short of an art form. Wide borders are alternated with narrower ones in infinite variations and the most highly prized jerseys have no two patterns repeated, and yet have patterns chosen to match and harmonise, so that the effect is rich but not garish. Descriptions of actual jerseys make this point more easily.

(a)   *A Fair Isle jersey from 1970*

9/2/9/2 repeated, with 10 or 11 different 9-row patterns (all of the 'continuous' type – waves, zigzags, diamonds, etc.), alternating with a small up-and-down 2-row pattern, and each pattern separated by 3 or 4 plain rows. Background colour is natural fawn throughout. The peerie pattern is Shetland black on fawn, and the larger pattern has 3 rows each of moorit, black and moorit on fawn.

A similar jersey, in shaded natural colours on a plain fawn ground, is 15/4/15/4 repeated, the 15-

row patterns being traditional Fair Isle *OXO* types, and the peerie patterns changing all the way up.

(b)   *A jersey knitted in Fair Isle around 1970*

15/4/9/4/15/4/9/4 repeated. The peerie patterns (4-row) are all different. The 15-row and 9-row patterns are also all different, though of matching styles. The peerie patterns are Shetland black on fawn, with 4 plain rows on each side (i.e. centred on a 12-row band of fawn). The larger patterns are all knitted in fawn on a background of moorit, black and moorit, with one extra plain row in moorit above and below. There is no transition between fawn ground and moorit ground.

(c)   *A prize-winning jersey knitted in Fetlar around 1930*

(1)//3/9/3//1/11/1//3/9/3//1/11/1 repeated. The 1-row and the 3-row pattern do not change throughout. Each 9-row pattern is different but in

A modern jersey using border patterns; the sleeve patterns have been knitted in reverse order!

the same 'continuous' style. Each 11-row pattern is a scaled-down version of a Fair Isle lozenge. Each of these patterns is separated from every other by 1 or 2 plain rows. The colours are entirely natural, with a mainly natural white ground, and the patterns use mainly moorit and medium fawn, with sparing use of Shetland black. This jersey is in the Shetland Museum collection.

(d)   A modern jersey knitted on Fair Isle

2/11/2/4/2/11/2/4 repeated. The little up-and-down 2-row pattern is used throughout. There are only two different 4-row and two different 11-row patterns which alternate. The 4-row patterns are continuous. The larger are of Fair Isle type, with small crosses. There are two plain rows between each.

(e)   A modern jersey knitted on Fair Isle

15/2/4/2/13/2/4/2 repeated. It begins with a Tree of Life, an effective touch. The larger patterns

here are of continuous type (joined diamonds, waves, etc.). There are 5 plain rows on each side of the 15- and 13-row patterns, and 3 on each side of the 4-row patterns. The background is mainly dark fawn. The 2-row pattern is black on fawn, the 4-row pattern moorit on fawn, and the larger patterns are white on moorit, white on black and white on moorit.

(f)   A pattern using larger stars

5/13/5/17/5/13/5/15/5/17/5/27/5/15/5 – this is the complete sequence. The last 5-row pattern is joined over the shoulder. Each pattern is different and unavoidable incomplete repeats are placed at the side. The large patterns are all stars of different types, with the largest across the yoke. This is very effective knitted in pastel natural shades (pink-fawn, blue-grey, white, etc.) on a dark ground. One plain row between patterns.

(g)   A modern Lerwick jersey

15/5/15/5 repeated, with no plain rows. A most intricate-looking result depending on good choice of patterns and a clever colour scheme. The 5-row peerie patterns vary throughout. The 15-row patterns are chosen to match from stars, flowers, etc. of equal repeat (one or two are repeated in sequence to make up the length required). Each 15-row motif is placed exactly above the preceding, and is joined by the same little joining devices.

The colour sequence adds to the unified effect. The large pattern is knitted in bands of pink-fawn on Shetland black, light fawn on moorit, and white on light grey in the centre row, repeated in reverse. The small pattern has 2 rows of medium fawn on black and a centre row of white on black.

Such careful planning can, of course, be omitted, as it is in one of the oldest Fair Isle jerseys known, where a great variety of patterns are knitted more or less at random and are united only by a common colour scheme. The shoulders in this old jersey, as well as the lower end of the sleeves, are filled in with 'blocks' (2 rows of 2&2, with a colour change every 4 rows) – an idea well worth bearing in mind for shoulder joins.

Norwegian Work

Large Stars (not all, incidentally, of Norwegian

A jersey knitted in Fair Isle in around 1970

Gansie knitted in Fair Isle and bought in Thurso c. *1914*
(NMAS)

origin) are the most recent addition to Shetland patterns. They are used today in fishermen's working gansies and panel jerseys, as well as being used to decorate gloves, mittens and ski caps.

(a)   The simplest type of gansie pattern using large stars has a patterned yoke, with body and sleeves quite plain (and probably machine knitted). This concentrates the hand-work and the warmth where they will be most useful, and is a feature shared with Scottish Fleet gansies.

(b)   For extra warmth the sleeves and body may be covered in seeding, a small allover pattern which keeps the second colour moving to keep the fabric double with the least effort. The stars in the yoke panel may be carried over to the tops of the sleeves and may be repeated just above the welt. Welt and cuffs may be decorated with a smaller but matching pattern.

The large stars which often make up the yoke pattern are generally framed between smaller bor-

Three Lerwick gansies: a simple yoked type (right) *and\ two panel jerseys*

Chart for a gansie yoke, knitted in red on black

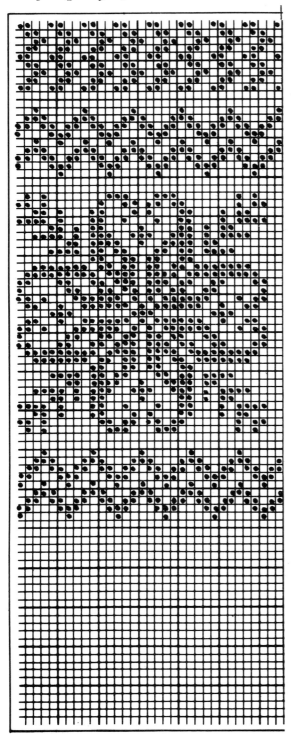

Chart for a Whalsay gansie in green on black

der patterns such as waves. The shoulders may be plain, or they may be joined by zig-zags, blocks or some other small and adaptable pattern.

Panel jerseys

If the star panel is placed vertically rather than horizontally, there is an immediate technical need to fill in the rest of the design by repeating the panel and filling in with seeding or with other panels, so that there is continuous patterning. This allows both wools to be carried right round each row. Here again there is enormous variety of design.

These panel jerseys look extremely complicated and, indeed, great skill often goes into placing the panels to best effect; for example, judging the armhole decreases so that a star panel runs neatly at the edge of the shoulder. Equally often this does not happen.

Many have two star panels running up on either side of the front and back, to join at the shoulder. If this join is properly planned, the pattern

'Export gansie' knitted in Skerries. Different blues on a white ground with fawn ribbing

becomes continuous over the shoulder. It thus follows that each panel contains either a whole number of stars (say, 5 or 6) or an extra half ($5\frac{1}{2}$ or $6\frac{1}{2}$), with the centre row of this last star grafted in to match. This involves great accuracy in estimating the number of rows needed for a required length.

The spaces under the arms and between panels are filled with seeding, or with other small panels, or with border patterns knitted vertically (as most can be) rather than horizontally.

Charts from two panel jerseys

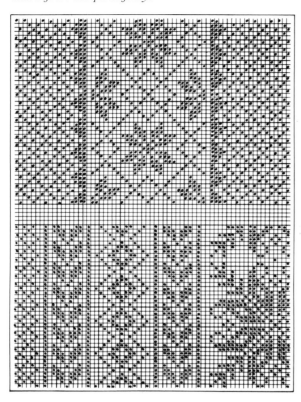

A jersey which illustrates the pattern

Modern panel jerseys

These are not intended as knitting instructions. Tension varies from knitter to knitter and from one batch of wool to the next, and must always be checked with the actual yarn to be used. These notes of actual jerseys are intended only to illustrate the gansie method.

(a) Cousin Steven's gansie

A boy's panel jersey knitted in Out Skerries, to fit size 87cm (34in). Tension approximately 8 stitches to 2½cm (1in) over the pattern.

Ribbing: 220 stitches are cast on and 30 rows in 1 & 1 rib knitted. Stitches are increased to 284 over 2 plain rows and the pattern set as follows: 23 for half of the seeding panel under the left arm; 29 for the left front star panel; 39 for the centre front seeded panel; 29 for the right front star panel; 45 for the right underarm seeded panel; 29 for the right back star panel; 39 for the centre back seeded panel; 29 for the left back star panel; and 22 for the remainder of the left underarm seeded panel.

The pattern is then knitted up, with each star occupying 25 rows plus 1 row between each repeat. It is repeated 3¼ times to the armhole opening, where 20 stitches are reduced under each arm and left on a stitch-holder. No further reductions, which gives a nice straight edge above the armhole. The star panel is not quite at the edge in this example.

The front has 5½ stars to the shoulder, joined to make a complete pattern. Front neck is shaped over the last 12 rows.

Sleeves: about 110 stitches are picked up or knitted up from the armhole edge, plus 20 from the under-arm reduction to make 130; the star panel is placed on the outside, with the rest filled by seeding; 5 stars are knitted. Cuff and neckband are double.

Colours: see Chapter 5.

(b) Cousin John's best gansie

Another Skerries jersey, to fit 107cm (42in).
Ribbing: 280 stitches are cast on and 8cm (3in) of 1 & 1 rib knitted. Stitches are then increased to 352

Charts from two panel jerseys

Charts from two panel jerseys

and the pattern set as in the previous example, though with differently sized panels. The main star panels at each side each cover 33 stitches, with the star itself being 31 stitches square. It is edged with 'Flags' knitted vertically and the centre front and back has three other small patterns arranged vertically in place of the more usual seeding. Underarm panels are filled with seeding. There are $5\frac{1}{2}$ stars to the shoulder join.

Colours: see Chapter 5.

(c) Panel jersey

This large jersey was knitted to fit 107–112cm (42–44in) chest. It has seven complete stars in each panel, and seeding under arms and centre front and back. Reductions at the armholes are planned from the start to match these panels – the final width between the arms of the finished jersey is the same as the width from the outside of one panel to the outside of the other at the lower edge; 6–8 stitches are also used for the armhole edge.

Ribbing: 280 stitches are cast on and $7\frac{1}{2}$cm (3in) of 1 & 1 rib knitted. The stitches are then increased to

328 in 1 round (roughly knit 6, make 1). The pattern is set: beginning centre underarm and allowing 43 for each star panel, 33 for centre front and centre back seeding and 45 for the underarm seeding (in other words, count 23, 43, 33, 43, 45, 43, 33, 43, 22).

At about 50cm ($19\frac{1}{2}$in) 18 stitches are put on a holder for underarm reduction at each side; further decreasing is done 10 times, making a total reduction on each side of 38 stitches. This leaves 7 to be knitted for the armhole edge.

Knitting is continued up to the shoulders, making some shaping for the front neck opening by reductions over the last 20 rows or so. 36 stitches centre front are kept on a stitch-holder and 10 more are reduced each side by knitting 2 together every second row for 20 rows.

The neckband is then knitted up from 56 stitches at the front and an equal number at the back (somewhere between 112 and 120 are needed).

The sleeve is knitted with a total of 120 stitches knitted up around the armhole edge, making a

A fine 'peaked' lumber, with corrugated rib   *Chart for waves and peaks*

neat edge with the outer edge of the star panel. Reductions are all centred underarm, small patterns being dropped as soon as incomplete, and the stars centred on top of the sleeve, down to around 64 stitches at the cuff. The cuff is 13cm (5in) of 2&2 rib.

The lumber method

Lumber jackets and other garments with front openings are knitted in exactly the same way as jerseys or gansies, with the addition of a **steek** centre front to allow for an opening (see also instructions for **buttonholes** and **buttonhole facing bands** in the next chapter on Knitting Techniques.)

The patterns must match in some way on either side of this opening, either by being symmetrical (which is usually most effective) or by continuing as though the opening were not there (which can look disjointed). In casting on there is also a slight difference from the gansie method in that the first stitches cast on are regarded as those of the right front, followed by those of the back and those of the left front. The join is thus centre front and, in

practice, will disappear when the opening is made.

Necklines of lumbers vary as do those of gansies, but are almost always shaped to make the front 2½–5cm (1–2in) or more below the back neck edge, which is generally left unshaped. Approximately one third of the stitches are used for the neck opening, or slightly more by some knitters.

Patterns for lumbers are often shared with gansies, panel lumbers being one example. Allover patterns are often used, particularly the diagonal type with stars or smaller fillings. There is more work in a lumber than in a jersey of the same size, and many are knitted for personal wear rather than for sale. There is thus very great individual variety in the patterns used.

Two are described here: the very popular Peaks and the rather interesting Sand Lodge type of pattern, both widely used for lumbers, though also suitable for gansies.

Lumbers with Peaks

The use of colour in Peaks (and Waves) is described in Chapter 5. They are a way of shading from a dark ground (with its pattern) to a light ground (with its pattern) and back. Two alternating patterns are generally used, though the same one, in different colour contrast, may be repeated. In the photograph the larger pattern is on the light ground, while the chart shows the larger pattern on the dark ground.

It will be noted from the chart that the diamonds or Peaks are not, in fact, square, but are knitted over 6 rows, with 1, 3, 5, 5, 3, 1 stitches respectively in each row. They therefore have a repeat along the row of 6 stitches and any pattern used looks very much more effective if it also has a repeat of 6 (or 12, or 18).

A typical peaked lumber

A typical peaked lumber to fit size 92–97cm (36–38in) is knitted as follows:
Ribbing: cast on 256 stitches plus 6–8 for the front opening, and rib for 7½cm (3in), in shade (1) 1 & 1 rib, or 12 rows in corrugated rib. Continue in shade (1) in stocking stitch and increase in the first row to 292 stitches, plus 6–8 for the steek.

The peaks are set in the third row by knitting 1 shade (2) every 6 stitches, placing the first coloured stitch immediately after the opening. The pattern continues as shown in the chart, with four vertical repetitions of the large star, three repetitions of the

Bottom

A Sand Lodge lumber knitted in Bressay

Chart for Sand Lodge type pattern. The lower motifs are interchangeable in any sequence

small star, and a small star centred over the shoulder.

Approximately 25 stitches are left on a stitch-holder to shape the armhole opening, and 6 more reduced gradually on each side thereafter. Shaping for the neck opening is done over the last 20 rows of the front, with none at the back.

The sleeve contains 132 stitches (it is comfortably wide) where knitted up from the armhole opening edge, and is reduced to approximately 90 at the cuff by decreasing 2 stitches every 6 rows or so.

A Sand Lodge lumber

The tension of this unusual lumber is about 8 stitches to 2½cm (1in). The pattern is very adaptable in a vertical scale.

There are five panels on each side of the front, and eleven at the back, with the stitches for the front opening (see **steek**) fitted in centre front. *Ribbing:* 240 stitches are cast on, and 15 rows in 1 & 1 rib knitted. These are eventually folded to the inside and hemmed (a neat edge is got by knitting

a purl row for the fold). The stitches are increased in one plain row to 280 (13 for each pattern, plus 6 for the front opening).

The pullover method

A V-necked pullover is best knitted in a flat piece after the armhole is reached, as it is not possible to use a steek to make a neck opening. The wool must be broken off at the neck edge at the end of every row and joined in again. A steek may still be used for the armholes, with some advantage. They, and the neck opening, should be finished off with a ribbed band, picked up in the same way as the sleeve stitches would otherwise be.

Magnie's diced pullover

Magnie recollects that this was knitted about 30 years ago by one of his sisters. It shows a very popular type and pattern.

The pattern repeat is 36 stitches. This and other variations may be found in the Pattern Notebook.

This type of pattern, with much use of the vari-

Close-up of a diced pattern

Magnie's diced pullover

ous fillings shown is also popular today for scarves (knitted in tubular fashion). Some shading of both colours is often introduced at the centre row or rows of the diamonds (see also Chapter 5 on colour).

Stockings

Any suitable stocking pattern may be decorated, either all over or with a fancy top. Good patterns for various suitable wools are to be found in many general knitting books and booklets (for example, Patons' *Woolcraft*). Fair Isle patterns are easy to adapt for tops, and the diced patterns are those generally used, without additional decoration, for kilt hose.

Stockings are no longer much knitted in Shetland, or elsewhere, but are a useful skill and an enjoyable pastime. They are done on four needles. Reductions at the back of the leg and for the toe should be done neatly and symmetrically, and the toe stitches should be grafted for a fine finish (see **decreasing, grafting, circular knitting**).

A good old stitch for the heel flap, which in effect gives double thickness when knitted in one colour is as follows:
Row 1: Slip 1 purlways, purl to end of row
Row 2: Slip 1 knitways, *knit 1; keeping yarn at back of work, slip 1 purlways, thus twisting the stitch. Repeat from *. Repeat these 2 rows as required.

Gloves and mittens

Once entirely patterned with small, allover patterns, most Shetland gloves and mittens now have a large star, or two, to fill the space on the back. There are many attractive refinements in finger patterns, thumb insets and palm patterns, given on the accompanying chart, and easier to follow from illustrations than from written instructions. Again, Patons' *Woolcraft* supplies many useful patterns for different wools, and a good method of setting in a thumb.

Gloves and mittens are often, these days, knitted without thumb gussets. This works well enough in

a mitten but shortens the life of a glove. Most methods of knitting gussets are similar to that described for gansie gussets, with regular increases on each side of an increasing number of stitches starting at the wrist. The edge is often outlined in one colour. Gloves can be tested for fit as the work progresses by being tried on.

In Shetland knitters make gloves, including fingers, as they are accustomed to knit everything else, on 35cm (14in) wires. Elsewhere, shorter needles are generally found more convenient.

Any holes which unavoidably develop around the fingers in gloves made by less experienced knitters may easily be darned from the inside. Usually all that is needed is a stitch to pull the wool tight.

Yoked jerseys

There are two main types today: the over-familiar, brightly-coloured Fair Isle type, which usually consists of various stars separated by Tree of Life patterns, set on a plain, machine-knitted body; and the Norwegian or Danish type. The advan-

Two pairs of mittens with typical patterns

Ladies' gloves. Note cuff and thumb gusset

An old pair of ladies' gloves

tage of incorporating the Tree is that it allows for regular reductions in every two rows without upsetting the pattern. The Norwegian type is not reduced so regularly and depends on the elasticity of knitting (which is quite considerable) for its fit. Various border patterns (often waves) are knitted in bands of perhaps 4–6cm (1½–2½in) with no reduction in the bands. All the reductions are done in the plain rows between patterns and quite considerable reductions in the number of stitches knitted can be made in one row without any gathering effect. The rate of reduction is nevertheless important.

Yoked jerseys, if knitted by hand, differ from the traditional gansie in that both body *and* sleeves are knitted from the bottom upwards, each part in circular fashion. When armhole level is reached on both body and sleeves, around 10 stitches (5cm or

2in) are put on holders at each centre underarm position. All the stitches are now put on the same needle (if a circular needle is used) or arranged on one set of needles (if a set of needles is used). The stitches from each sleeve must be fitted into the small space left by the 10 or so stitches taken off to begin the underarm shaping on each side, and the first few rows may be a tight fit.

Patterning may begin as soon as all stitches are on one round. It is useful to keep a note of stitches and reductions.

Instructions for yokes again depend on the wool used and other factors, but the depth of the yoke can be estimated by measuring from neck edge to the level on the outer arm corresponding to the armpit in the inside and, by calculating from the known tension, an estimate of the number of rows will be got.

Chart of glove and mitten patterns, formerly used back and front, now restricted to palms

Chart of glove patterns for thumbs, fingers and cuffs

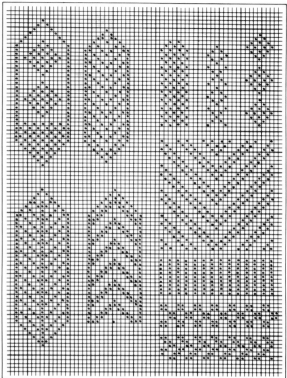

Some indication of yoke sizes (at maximum width) when knitted in 2-ply Shetland yarn are:

71cm (28in)	208 stitches
77cm (30in)	225 stitches
82cm (32in)	240 stitches
87cm (34in)	255 stitches
92cm (36in)	268 stitches

and so on, with a tension of around 7·5 stitches to 2½cm (1in).

The neck edge should be approximately 95–100 stitches for a lady's jersey, and 120 stitches for a man's. Reductions should be fitted in to plain rows every 10 rows or so, though smaller or larger bands can be knitted.

There is great scope for new designs in this type of jersey.

Tammies

The 'tammy', abbreviated from the Tam o' Shanter (after Burns's bibulous hero), became popular wear for young ladies in later Victorian times. The Fair Isle version had a long popularity. One is shown here, with a neat eight-part crown.

It is an interesting point that it is knitted not from brim to crown, but in reverse. Invisible increasing is neater than any form of decreasing; hence its very tidy appearance.

Generally today stitches are cast on for the brim; there is a short ribbed band; the pattern is introduced and stitches are increased to the widest part, and then reduced to form the crown. Some have continuous increasing and decreasing; others fit any change of size into plain rows between narrow bands of different patterns, as is also done for some yoked jerseys. Some have little shaping between the brim and the beginning of the wheel pattern, relying on dressing to give the tammy its shape by stretching the knitting.

Double decreasing is used for the ornamental reductions.

The finished tammy, however knitted, is dressed on a suitably-sized plate or piece of firm card, and should lie flat.

Seven wheel pattern tammies

Yoked jerseys (The Shetland Woollen Specialists, Edinburgh)

Old stockings, probably knitted in Fair Isle, with old allover pattern (NMAS)

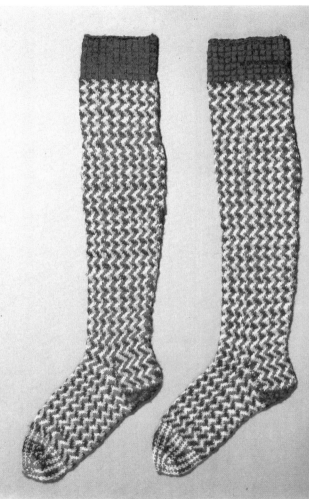

Skullcaps

Skullcaps are popular and new. They are similar to tammies but are close-fitting, knitted quite straight for 10–12cm (4–5in), and then neatly reduced with a fancy crown of some kind. Planning a pattern for the border is similar to the method for a ski cap, and the crown can be done in any way so long as it fits. It is not required to be as flat as that of a tammy, and can therefore be reduced more slowly.

A typical adult size might have 140 stitches cast on, and eight rows in 2&2 **corrugated rib** for firmness at the edge. The stitches are then increased to 160 by regular increases in the first plain row, and a pattern introduced, for example a 5/13/5 arrangement, with one plain row between patterns. The small pattern might be knitted 16 times in the round (10 stitches per repeat) and the large one fitted in 8 times (20 stitches per repeat).

The crown can be reduced in five sections, with a double decrease at each 'corner' in every second round.

Fair Isle tammy (Shetland Museum)

Quantities of wool required

The quantities of wool required for any garment are impossible to predict, as they will vary according to the colour scheme. The only way to know how much is needed would be to weigh the different colours before starting, and weigh them again when finished, the difference being the wool used. Unless one wants to repeat a pattern exactly, this serves little purpose.

As a very rough guide, a man's gansie in a small size might require 500–600gm (approximately 18–22oz) of 2-ply Shetland jumper yarn, with perhaps half of this weight in a panel jersey being the background colour. The weight will depend on the closeness of the knitting, and the proportions of different colours will depend entirely on the design. A lady's lumber of medium size uses approximately 400–500gm (16–18oz). A lumber with peaks will use larger amounts of the two main ground colours, lesser but significant amounts of the shading colours for the peaks, and modest amounts of any contrast used.

A stranded jersey will always use considerably more wool than a plain jersey of the same size, as much of the fabric is, in effect, double. The extra amount will again depend on the style, in particular on the number of plain, unpatterned rows used, but can be 50 per cent or more.

4 Knitting Techniques

Some knitters may find these helpful; many knitters will already be familiar with these techniques, and many will have their own, and possibly better methods. Only a few are essential to good stranded knitting; circular knitting is the basic technique to master, but not at all a difficult one, and grafting is useful for a professional finish.

Buttonholes

Calculate first how long the work is to be and how many buttons will be needed.

To make a small buttonhole, suitable for a lady's cardigan or lumber, pass the wool over the needle and knit the next 2 stitches together.

To make a larger, horizontal hole, cast off the required number of stitches according to the tension worked, and continue the round. On the next round, cast on the same number of stitches, turning the work to the purl side as necessary, and continue to knit round.

Buttonhole facing bands. These are normally faced with ribbon, which should be quite firm, non-shrink, and wide enough to cover the buttonholes with a little to spare. There must also be 2–3 stitches allowed to make an edge to be turned in. Hem down this edge tacking on the ribbon at the same time and turning in top and bottom edges neatly. Cut through ribbon to make a hole corresponding to each buttonhole and oversew by hand or by machine. A band will also normally be required on the other side to give a firm base for the buttons.

A knitted band may also be knitted in 1 & 1 rib or moss stitch and sewn on separately to accommodate both buttons and buttonholes. If this is knitted before the neckband, the stitches remaining at the top of both sides can be added to those picked up round the neck edge for the neckband (or collar) and knitted together with them.

Some knitters use a very fine wire (size 16) to pick up stitches along the entire edge of the work and knit the band at right angles to the rest of the cardigan. This requires some skill both in making a neat edge (again, there must be 2–3 stitches allowed) and in calculating tension accurately to ensure that the band will lie flat. It does however give a more elastic edge than the sewn band.

Casting off

Shetland knitters avoid casting off where possible, preferring to graft, or keeping stitches on a stitch-holder to be joined in again (e.g. armhole reductions; centre back or front neckband).

Suspended cast-off is good for polo necks: knit 2, slip first over second (as in normal casting off), *return second stitch from right-hand needle to left-hand needle, and knit this and the next stitch together, knit one*. Repeat from * to *

Casting off together can be used for shoulder seams, where it gives a firmer join than grafting. Place back and front shoulder stitches together on their pins, with right side of work inside (wrong side facing) and use a knitting needle in the right hand, one size larger than the two holding the stitches. Put this third needle into the back of the first stitch on the front needle and the front of the first stitch on the back needle and knit together. Repeat and cast off from the right-hand needle in the usual way.

The stitches of the front should be kept on a pin until the back is finished.

Casting on

There are many ways of casting on.

Cable cast on in three stages

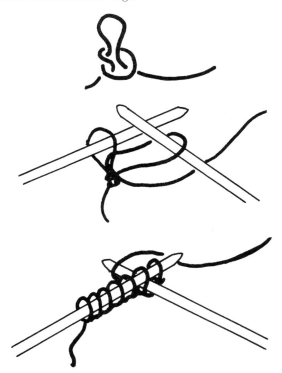

Circular Needles: (a) *Casting on,* (b) *Knitting the first row; reverse the work and knit into the first stitch cast on. Take care the work is not twisted*

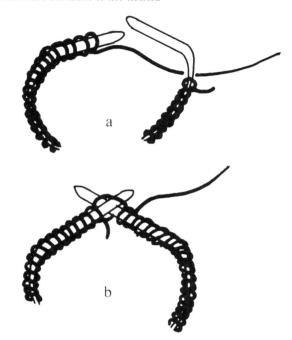

Cable cast on gives a good edge. Two needles are used and the first loop made with a slip stitch and placed on the left-hand needle. The second loop is made by knitting through this loop in the normal way. Third and subsequent loops are made by withdrawing the right-hand needle completely each time and reinserting it between the two previous stitches.

Make sure the cast-on stitches are not twisted before knitting the second round.

Machine-knitted welts often have a rather thin, weak edge. This can be overcome by making a double edge, folding the ribbing in two and joining it in at the point where the pattern starts.

Choice of wool

The colour schemes given here all rely on a supply of wool in the natural colours. Stockists of Shetland wool are given at the end of the book.

However, almost any kind of fairly plain wool can be used, if it has a suitable colour range. Thicker wool in natural colours is increasingly available, and can be most effective with the smaller patterns. Working jerseys are better knitted in synthetic yarn in dark colours.

Circular knitting

Circular knitting is the only real secret of successful Fair Isle knitting. It makes manipulation of two wools a relatively easy matter and puts Fair Isle knitting within reach of any competent knitter. Until quite recently it was the only known way of knitting, but is now used more on the Continent of Europe and in Shetland than in mainland Britain. It is still used by many people for small items such as gloves and socks, but is also useful for jerseys. It is quite essential to use circular knitting for stranded knitting. Everything is then knitted in plain stitch, with the yarn not in use lying loosely on the inside of the work. Shetland knitters *never* knit in purl when using two wools, preferring to break off their yarns at the end of each row and rejoin them at the beginning of the next if there is no other way of doing it, as above the 'V' opening in a V-necked pullover.

Needles may be circular nylon one-piece needles, such as Aero Twinpins, or a set of four double-ended stocking needles of suitable length. The shorter lengths of circular needle are, generally speaking, the most useful. If the needle is too long, the knitting may be too short to reach round it.

Circular needles are smooth, strong and can also be used for flat knitting. They hold the stitches securely and have replaced sets of four needles in Faeroe and Denmark. Shetland knitters use sets of four needles, generally 35cm (14in) in length, even for small-scale work such as glove fingers, but most other knitters will find a selection of shorter lengths more easy to work with. As stitches tend to fall off these needles as the work moves round, they should be long enough to hold the maximum number of stitches planned comfortably.

Shetland knitters keep their knitting secure and rigid by use of a knitting belt. The end of the right-hand needle can also be stuck into an ordinary belt. Sometimes only three needles are used to maintain rigidity and the end of the knitting may be pulled down firmly and tied round the belt. They use the Continental method of knitting and can achieve great speed, but this method is not easy to learn if the English knitting method has been learned previously, nor is it necessary to try to copy it.

Cast on in the usual fashion if using a circular needle. If you are using a set of four, move the stitches from needle to needle as they fill up, ending with an even distribution on three, with one left to work with. Begin the first round by knitting into the first stitch cast on. Make sure at

Shetland knitter with long wires and knitting belt

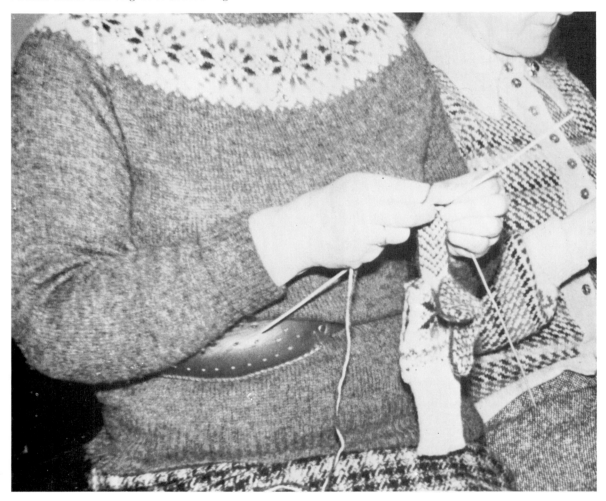

this point that the work is not twisted. Insert a coloured marker (a short strand of contrasting wool knitted into the work) to mark the point where the round begins and where the pattern will change.

When adapting a jersey pattern for circular knitting one simply adds together the stitches for front and back and casts them all on at once. There are no side seams. In case the original pattern has allowed for seams, it is wise to check tension carefully before starting. In Fair Isle gansie knitting there is no shaping in the body of the jersey. There is normally no problem if shaping is required; everything is knitted with the right side facing and increases under the arms or decreases elsewhere may be incorporated.

With a gansie shape the body is knitted first, armholes are made, the shoulders joined, and the sleeves then knitted down towards the wrist from stitches picked up round the armhole opening. With a yoked jersey the body is knitted up to the beginning of the armhole (where some reductions may be made), sleeves are knitted up to the same level (and a similar reduction made), and at that point all stitches are put in order on the one needle: front, right sleeve, back and left sleeve. It can be difficult for the first few rows to accommodate the sleeve stitches in the space available on the circular needle. The yoke pattern may be introduced at any point after all stitches are on the one needle.

Gansie method

Yoked jersey method

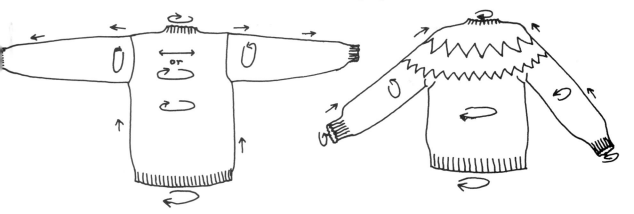

Continental knitting

The wool is controlled by the left hand, as in crochet. It is pulled taut behind the working loop on the left-hand needle and simply pulled through this by the right-hand needle, on which it remains. Beginners will find it a little difficult to control the tension with this method until they are used to it but, with practice, it is very quick and explains the phenomenal speed of Shetland knitters, who can reach 200 stitches a minute.

Continental knitting combines well with English knitting (where the wool is held in the right hand) for stranded knitting, as it allows one colour to be held in each hand. It is, however, not an essential skill, as both wools can be controlled by the right hand.

Continental knitting

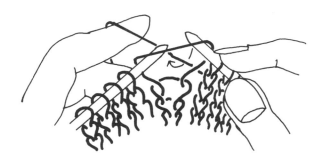

Decreasing

As gansies are unshaped in the body, decreasing is used only in the sleeves. **Double decreasing** (see below) is used on crowns of tammies and ski caps,

and at the centre-front of neckbands on V-necked pullovers and jerseys.

To make a decrease which slopes to the right, knit 2 together by inserting the right-hand needle into the second loop on the left-hand needle, through it into the first loop, and knit 2 together with an ordinary plain stitch.

To make a decrease which slopes to the left, insert the right-hand needle through the backs of the first and second loops on the left-hand needle and knit 2 together. Alternately, slip 1, knit 1 and pass the slipped stitch over the knitted stitch. These give very similar results.

It is attractive to reduce in pairs, one sloping left and one right, on either side of a centre stitch or number of stitches under a sleeve or down the back of hose. On the right, slope to the left and on the left slope to the right.

Double decreasing is necessary to reduce rapidly on crowns of tammies, etc. There are various methods with differing effects, none of which are wrong:

(a) Slip 1, knit 2 together, pass the slipped stitch over the knitted stitch and drop it off.
(b) Knit 3 together.
(c) A more elegant version of (b): before knitting 3 together, rearrange them with the centre stitch on top (there is no particularly easy way of doing this). This gives a ribbed effect, with one dominant stitch and the reductions tucked neatly behind it.

Grafting

Grafting is a way of joining two sets of stitches by darning in a thread with a sewing needle to imitate a row of knitted stitches. The two pieces then

Grafting

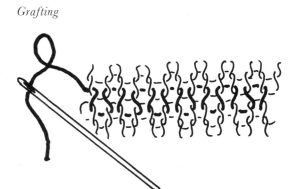

Lifted increase

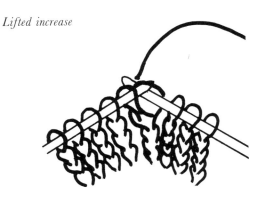

look continuous. The join is quite flat and in-visible, and is used over the shoulder of a jersey or lumber and at the toe of a sock.

The work is done with the two edges to be joined lined up on their respective knitting needles. It is easier to judge results by keeping the right sides uppermost. Use a piece of matching yarn about four times the length of the seam to be made, and thread this on to a darning needle or bodkin.

This thread must imitate knitted stitches and thus loops in and out of each stitch twice. It must come up through the first loop on needle A (as its first thread); down through the first loop on needle B (as its second thread); up through the second loop on needle B (as its first thread); down through the first loop on needle A (as its second thread); up through the second loop on needle A (as its first thread); down through the second loop on needle B (as its second thread); and so on.

Increasing

Although there is seldom shaping in a jersey of Shetland type, the welt is generally knitted to be tighter than the rest of the work. This can be achieved by knitting it with a needle one size smaller than that required for the body and by increasing by a variable amount in the plain row between rib and pattern. This amount varies with fashion but currently is about 1 stitch in 10.

Increases are also used when knitting sleeves for yoked jerseys (from wrist to armhole), in gussets in jerseys and gloves, and in tammies between the rim and the widest part.

(a) The neatest method is the 'Lifted Increase'. Knit into the stitch below the next stitch which would normally be knitted, using it as though it were an extra stitch. It will stretch

up quite easily to fit in and will be almost invisible.

(b) Knit into the length of yarn between two stit-ches, twisting this to avoid making a hole, which can be difficult to avoid with this method.

(c) Knit into the front and back of same stitch, the yarn all the time remaining behind the work. This produces a bar.

Joining yarn

Where possible join in new wool at the beginning of a round. Otherwise join it by unravelling a few inches of the old ball and a few inches at the beginning of the new ball, and twist half of each together, leaving the unused half to be darned in later. Knit with the spliced length for 4–5 stitches.

Picking up stitches

It is often necessary to pick up stitches to knit a neckband, a button band, the sleeves on a jersey, or the heel of a sock. These should not be picked up too near the edge or loops will result. They should be evenly spaced without large gaps. The natural elasticity of knitting helps to space them out, as does the use of a needle finer than that to be used for the actual knitting. In Shetland a size 16 wire is used to pick up the first row. It helps to cast off as little as possible – the stitches at the back (and sometimes centre front) of a jersey may be left on a stitch-holder and used directly for the band.

Ribbing

Use of ribbing in Shetland jerseys has varied with fashion. The earliest gansies have none and as a result lack fit and shape. The fashion for a while was for a deep welt. Today many knitters have revived an old style of ribbing, described by Mary

Thomas as 'corrugated ribbing'. It is rather inelastic but gives a nice, firm edge and a suitable finishing touch to an allover jersey. It can be used for welt, cuffs, neckband and front band. A modern short-cut, machine-knitted ribbing, is to be deplored when used on an allover jersey – it is always the part that wears out first.

Corrugated ribbing is done with one dominant colour for the plain stitches and the various shades which appear in the jersey used in turn for the purl stitches. Sometimes only one contrasting colour is used, and indeed it is possible to knit this type of rib with two balls of the same colour. Even 2·5cm (1in) gives a good edge.

Ribbing is generally done with a needle one size smaller than that used for the patterned part of the jersey, e.g. size 13 for the rib and size 11 or 12 for the jersey (British sizes).

Shaping

The only shaping in an allover jersey is usually just above the welt and down the inside of the arm. The elasticity of knitting adapts very well to the human shape without undue shaping.

Shaping of yokes and tammies (berets) can be done regularly, say, every two rounds, by using the type of pattern which allows this – Star and Tree for a yoke; Wheel pattern for a tammy. It is also possible to knit either a yoke or a tammy in small bands of different patterns, each perhaps 2–4cm (1–2in) in depth, with all the necessary reductions being done in the plain row between pattern bands. It is not possible to reduce regularly in this type of pattern without spoiling it, but this is in fact not at all necessary, as the knitting will stretch and gather up imperceptibly to fit. This adaptability gives the designer great scope.

Armhole openings are often shaped by casting off (or putting aside on a stitch-holder) 5–7·5cm (2–3in), and further reducing on either side to a total overall of around 10cm (4in) maximum. This is generally done today, but is a question of modern taste for fitted shoulders. Traditional gansies (in common with modern Norwegian, Faeroese and other ethnic jerseys) were not shaped at all. This resulted in a dropped shoulder line. If reduction around the armhole is overdone, it will result in the sleeve being out of line when the stitches are picked up. The most satisfactory method of reducing seems to be to reduce as rapidly as possible, within 6–8 rows of beginning the armhole opening, and thereafter to knit the armhole with a straight edge.

Steek

This old Scots word is usually translated as 'stitch' but has connotations of 'stick' or 'fasten tightly' (to 'steek a yett' is to shut a gate, so that it is difficult to open again). Hence its Shetland application to the various methods used to prepare the front opening on a lumber jacket or cardigan, or the armhole opening. Different knitters have different methods, and there is room here for experiment, as even good Mainland knitters puzzle over the superior methods of knitters from other parts!

In former days, as still in Faeroe, knitwear was fulled or felted, and cutting it to fashion it into a jacket posed no problems – the untidy cut edge could be bound with braid but was not in danger of unravelling. Today we prefer our woollies unfelted, and considerable precautions have to be taken before cutting up the front of a garment to make an opening.

One method which I have not come across in Shetland, but which is quite simple, is to wind both yarns several times round the needle at each round, fairly loosely, so that they pass round the needle without obstruction, and drop these off in the course of the next round while making a new set. This leaves a ladder of wide loops which can be cut up centre and tied off or darned in. A stitch or two should be left spare on each side (before the pattern proper is taken up again) to allow for picking up the band or sewing on a ribbon.

Another simple method is to leave 6 stitches extra between pattern stitches (nervous knitters may prefer to leave more): e.g. 1 background colour, 1 pattern, 2 background, 1 pattern, 1 background. All ends must be knotted and finished off and darned in or oversewn lengthwise. These extra 6 or 8 stitches should be knitted tightly.

Some knitters knit a steek in moss stitch.

Some knitters have a method which involves knitting 2 together and making a new stitch three or four times in every steek; this prevents the stitches running when cut. Other remarks apply. The most laborious method involves unravelling a length of wool and darning it in.

Stranded knitting

Stranded knitting can be defined as knitting with two colours, a pattern colour and a ground colour in the same row, and stranding the wool not in use loosely along the back or wrong side of the work. It is not woven in by winding round the working yarn except very exceptionally. This technique is widely used, not only in Shetland and Fair Isle, but also in Faeroe, Iceland, Norway, Finland, Estonia, Turkey, Peru and elsewhere.

The patterns are carefully selected and planned to avoid large stretches in one colour, about 7 stitches (2½cm or 1in) in Jumper Yarn seldom being exceeded. The resting wool is laid without pulling along the inside of the work, where the naturally felty nature of most wool, particularly Shetland wool, keeps it in place.

When knitting with two colours Shetlanders use both hands, with a combination of the Continental (left-handed) and the British (right-handed) methods of knitting. It is equally possible, though slower, to hold both wools in the right hand, one on first and one on second fingers, or even on one finger only, picking up and dropping as required. The important thing is to keep knitting in circular fashion, in plain stitch, and avoid pulling the wool tightly at any point. Shetland knitters prefer the circular method *not* because they are so expert but because it is so easy!

Tension

Tension is perhaps second only to the circular method as a basic concept. A sample of reasonable dimensions must be knitted with the wool chosen before embarking on any larger piece. (This can serve the additional purpose of testing colour schemes). It must be patterned, and the tension must be read off as so many stitches and so many rows to some suitable distance, say, 5cm (2in). Printed patterns can give some indication of size of needles preferred and the best tension to aim for (as knitting must be neither too tight nor too loose), but any careful knitter should be able to adapt a pattern to their own use by checking their tension against the measurements required.

With Shetland 2-ply Jumper yarn, to take one example, most knitters work with needle size 10 over the patterned part (using size 12 for the rib), with a tension of approximately 7 stitches to 2½cm (or 7 stitches to 1in). This might vary with the quality of the yarn, up to 7½ or 8 stitches, and must be checked very carefully.

If a jersey is planned to fit a chest measurement of 90cm (almost 36in) actual size, it might need to be knitted 5cm (2in) larger for a comfortable fit, giving 95cm (38in).

At 7 stitches to 2½cm (1in) this would require 266 stitches. At 7½ stitches to 2½cm (1in), it would require 285 stitches. At 8 stitches to 2½cm (1in), it would require 304 stitches. This shows the considerable difference for a comparatively small difference in tension.

There is no way to know one's tension other than by careful measurement of samples and by trial and error thereafter.

If tension has to be adjusted, a size larger or a size smaller needle should be tried, again working with a new sample of at least 30–40 stitches and as many rows of pattern.

From the tension we can calculate the number of stitches needed over the patterned part and thus choose or select patterns which will fit in neatly. It is not always possible to have a perfect fit, but any join should be under one arm and as inconspicuous as possible. Ideally patterns should be centred back and front, with no incomplete patterns.

Washing and dressing

Shetland wool (including most wool commonly described as Shetland) has a tendency to shrink and felt, and must be washed carefully. This is especially important with allover jerseys, with their extra thickness and weight of wool.

Before washing, the neck edge should be gathered with a string or thread to prevent it stretching and any front opening should be carefully tacked together.

Garments should be washed by hand in warm water with a mild soap, and rinsed very thoroughly, also using only lukewarm or tepid water. They should then be squeezed as dry as possible or spun-dry in a thin bag to prevent undue stretching. On no account should they be tumble-dried. They may be stretched flat on a towel or suitable flat surface (a fine frame or mesh speeds the drying process) or stretched to dry on a 'woolly board'. Boarding a jersey is always done before it reaches the customer and gives even an old jersey a new lease of life.

As Shetland jerseys are basically square, with the sleeves at right angles to the body, a woolly board can be any flat square board of the right size, over which the jersey can be stretched. One long pole can support the sleeves with two shorter

Child's jersey on a woolly board

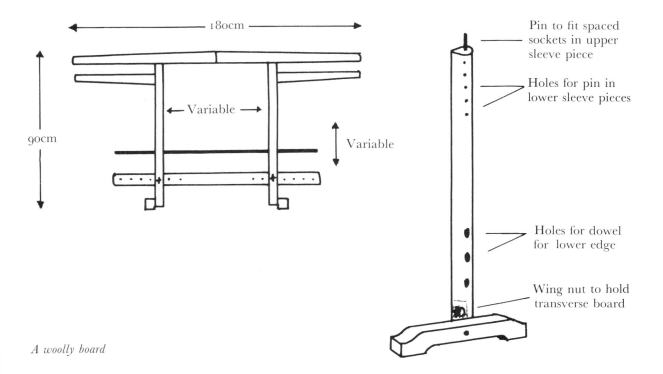

A woolly board

180cm

Variable

Variable

90cm

Pin to fit spaced sockets in upper sleeve piece

Holes for pin in lower sleeve pieces

Holes for dowel for lower edge

Wing nut to hold transverse board

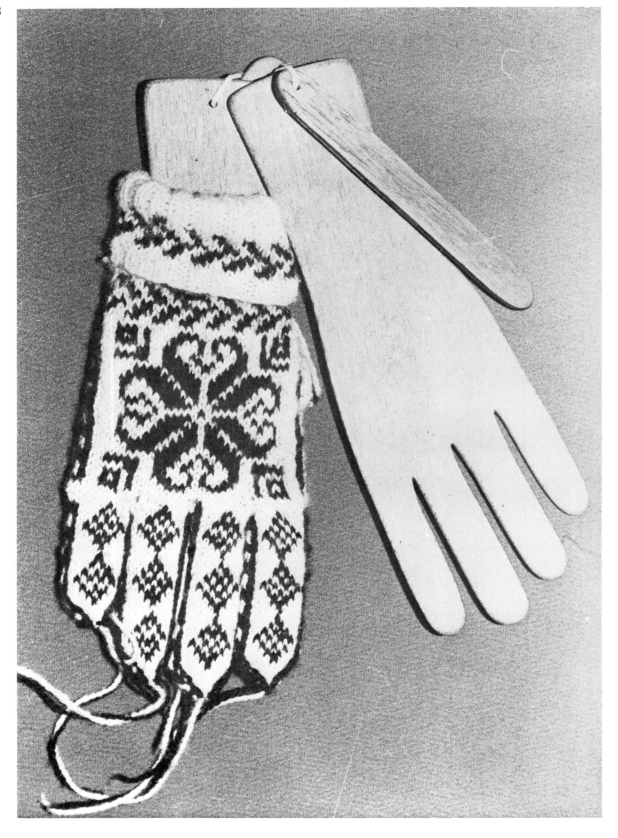

Dressing a new glove

ones to stretch them down. The lower edges should be clipped together – clothes-pegs work well for this. There are many adjustable types of board, most with feet, and some suitable frames can also be bought.

Gloves benefit from being dried on a glove board, which is glove-shaped with four fingers and a separate piece for the thumb. In the past boards were also made for stockings, tammies, long johns, and other things, and shawls are still dressed by pegging out on grass or tying on to a frame. Any special item such as a hand-knitted skirt would benefit from having a board made for it.

Do not be afraid to stretch a jersey quite firmly when fitting it on to a frame. It can then be left anywhere suitable to dry, indoors and out, without fear of shrinking.

The rib will stretch with the jersey and will need to be revived, particularly if machine-knitted. Steam very gently with a damp cloth and a warm iron, keeping the iron away from the knitting so that no pressure is applied and lifting the cloth quickly to allow it to dry out.

If jerseys must be hung up to dry it is better to hang them folded down the centre, with one sleeve hanging down each side, than to peg them up, which stretches them out of shape.

5 The Use of Colour in Fair Isle Knitting

Shetland knitters have always had a variety of colours available, both from the native sheep and from the local vegetable dyes used for dyeing tweed and blankets long before knitting developed.

Shetland sheep are a very old breed with several special features. Their ancient origin is vouched for by their short tails and their wool is amongst the finest and softest known. They also exist in a great variety of colours. Although today most are white, this is a recent change. Until quite recently there was a high proportion of coloured sheep and many speckled or part-coloured sheep, with fleeces like those of Jacob's sheep today. The most valued colours were Shetland black (a very dark brown), moorit (a rich russet) and grey, as well as white, and these colours are still fostered by the Breed Society as well as being very popular with knitters.

The local vegetable dyes were in use from the earliest times. Many well-known dye plants are found in Shetland. Lichen was used to produce a russet or brown shade, and the bog-ore method was used for black. Many other dyes were known which gave good yellows, a pale blue, dark green and a pinky-red.

These local vegetable dyes were largely replaced in Shetland between 1820 and 1840 by imported vegetable dyes such as madder, logwood and indigo. Indigo, in particular, was rare and a difficult dye to use, but these new dyes were so much clearer and brighter than the old ones that their popularity is easy to understand.

There was no essential change in the relationship between the Shetlander and her dye pot until the introduction of chemical dyes. These were brighter, faster and easier to use than any of the old recipes. The wealth of colour so suddenly made available was not always used wisely but the early experiments paved the way for the mastery of colour which today marks the Shetland knitter.

Today there are excellent ranges of colours available in mill-dyed wool, both natural and dyed shades. My only criticism is that there is for some reason no red to match the old madder of Fair Isle and no blue to match their indigo. Those planning to work with Shetland wool will find it useful to acquire their own stock of different colours (see the list of stockists at the end of the book). It is useful also to remember that slight differences in shade between batches from different dye baths will be less noticeable in patterned work, and even small remnants of wool can be used. The colour schemes given in this chapter are only a small sample of schemes devised by modern Shetland knitters. All the schemes can be used with ground and pattern colours reversed. In general it pays to be cautious in the use of colour, and to try out several small trial pieces before launching into a major work.

Working with colour

Only two colours are used in any one row or round. Some simple colour schemes use only two colours throughout while some very sophisticated ones change both colours very frequently. Quite surprising effects can be got from quite simple variations and experimentation is always to be encouraged. The only guiding principle which almost amounts to a rule is that the pattern will remain most distinct if the level of contrast between background colour and pattern colour is kept as constant as possible through whichever changes are made. Many of the examples given in this chapter show this very clearly.

These examples bring out one other favourite trick of Shetland knitters: a special emphasis on the colour scheme chosen for the centre row or rows (indicated as C).

Otherwise choice of colour depends on the taste of the knitter. Sibyl I. Matthews in *Needle-Made Rugs* expressed several sound ideas, which could have been those of any expert Shetland knitter:

> It is nearly always wise to introduce a small amount of an odd colour into a sober colour scheme; conversely, a neutral colour can tone down a too-bright one. Contrast is just as desirable as harmony but needs greater skill. . . . Black should be used with great discrimination. Generally speaking, very dark brown produces far better results than black would do.

Shetland knitters today like to work with natural shades. Levels of contrast are easier to control with greys and browns than between such dyed shades as orange and green. They too tend to avoid dyed black or bleached white except for special effects, using instead dark brown or natural white. However, every new project gives the opportunity to try a new blend of colours.

The oldest colour schemes, those from Fair Isle, have already been mentioned. Patterns were knitted in bands of red and white alternating with bands of blue (or dark brown) and gold. The red/blue/red ground sequence was followed quite strictly and the pattern, formed by the white and gold stitches, stood out clearly. The change of colour sometimes seems to have had little connection with the pattern being knitted! The larger patterns were, however, usually knitted in three bands of 5 or 6 rows each.

Today changes of colour are usually symmetrical, with special treatment of the centre row if the pattern is large enough to allow this. To give a very simple example, which also shows how levels of contrast are kept similar through changes of ground and pattern colour, a pattern might be knitted in bands of moorit on natural black, dark fawn on moorit, white on medium fawn (C), dark fawn on moorit and moorit on natural black. The centre row itself might be knitted in dark grey on black, between two bands of white on medium fawn, with no loss of continuity to the eye.

Gansie colour schemes are among the simplest and need little explanation. Most working gansies are dark and use only two colours; for example, a pattern knitted in red or turquoise on black or in light blue on navy blue. The fancier gansies for dress occasions or for customers in Lerwick or elsewhere usually have a light background in white or natural, with the pattern knitted in shades of blue and brown. Possibly to reduce the amount of work involved in gansies knitted for export, the ground is seldom shaded – there is no technical reason for this – and the level of contrast thus varies, often giving a striped appearance. Indeed, if the pattern colour is shaded too closely to the ground colour, the pattern can apparently disappear in places. It is enough to change the ground from white to natural behind the darker colours to avoid this.

In the following examples (C) indicates the colour scheme for the centre row or rows. As all these schemes are symmetrical they are repeated in reverse from (C) to the beginning.

(a) A panel jersey from the Out Skerries

The background is entirely white with the star panels and seeding knitted as follows:

4 rows dark blue; 4 rows medium blue; 4 rows light blue; 1 row navy (C); 4 rows light blue; 4 rows medium blue; 4 rows dark blue. 1 row medium blue between stars to make up pattern (stars 25 rows).

(b) A panel jersey from the Out Skerries

The rib is fawn as are neckband and cuffs. Ground to the pattern is entirely white. The stars and seeding are as follows:

1 row black; 2 rows royal blue; 2 rows medium blue; 3 rows light blue; 2 rows grey-blue; 2 rows medium blue; 2 rows royal blue; 3 rows black (C); repeat in reverse order for complete sequence (33 rows).

(c) A border pattern from a ski cap (5/13/5)

Ribbing and ground in natural medium fawn.

5-row pattern: 5 rows medium grey on medium fawn. 1 row medium fawn between patterns.

13-row pattern: 3 rows moorit on natural white; 2 rows dark grey on medium or light fawn; 3 rows Shetland black on light grey (C); 2 rows dark grey on medium or light fawn; 3 rows moorit on natural white.

(d) A colour scheme for a diced pattern

This was used on a tammy, but would be equally useful for a pullover or jersey. The colours are reversed in alternate sections (ground colour being used for pattern colour and vice versa). The effect is thus more complex than the number of colours used would indicate. The first row given is the first row of the diamond with the darker ground, but will also be that of the centre row of the adjoining diamond with the light ground, the colours being reversed in use.

1 row grey and Shetland black; 1 row dyed medium fawn and dark grey; 2 rows natural white and dark fawn; 3 rows natural white and moorit; 1 row dyed fawn and dark grey; 1 row grey and Shetland black (C); 1 row dyed fawn and dark grey; 3 rows white and moorit; 2 rows white and dark fawn; 1 row dyed fawn and dark grey; 1 row grey and Shetland black (the first row of the next repeat).

(e) Mike's jersey

This nice old pullover was knitted in Lerwick around 1950. It has a diagonal allover pattern and a simple but effective colour scheme over a 16-row repeat.

3 rows fawn on Shetland black; 5 rows natural on Shetland black; 3 rows moorit on Shetland black; 5 rows natural on Shetland black.

BREED OF THE ZETLAND AND ORKNEY ISLANDS.

Ram 3 Years old, of the Ancient Breed, from the Isle of Enhallow. Ewe 3 Years old from the Island of Rousay.

bred by William Traill Esq.r of Woodwick. The Lamb a cross of the pure Cheviot.

Published April 1840, by Longman Orme Brown, Green & Longmans Paternoster Row, London.

A print of 1840 showing the native sheep of Shetland and Orkney (NMAS)

Peaks and Waves

Peaks are a popular way of shading the ground from very light to very dark, as has already been mentioned in Chapter 3, where a chart for the different colours is also given. Waves shade the background in exactly the same way but give a less effective result and are thus less popular. The colours used are usually only four though more are available in the range of 2-ply Shetland jumper wool and may be used. Possible sequences would be:

1 Shetland black, with pattern, moorit, medium fawn, light fawn (with pattern);
2 Moorit (with pattern), medium fawn, light fawn, natural white (with pattern);
3 Navy blue, medium blue, light blue, dyed white (with pattern);
4 Bottle green, medium green, light green, lemon yellow or light fawn (with pattern).

The patterns themselves, and their background colours, are also often shaded; a bright contrast is usually introduced into the centre row of each. For example, a border pattern knitted on the light ground might be shaded from dark brown through moorit to light fawn (C) and the ground behind always light but shaded slightly behind the black, perhaps with pale orange for contrast. A star knitted on the dark ground might shade from tangerine to white (C) with the centre row or rows knitted on a rust ground.

(f) An allover jersey with peaks in green

In this jersey, the larger pattern is knitted on the dark green ground as follows:

2 rows orange on dark green; 2 rows fawn on green; 2 rows mustard on black; 1 row pale blue on tan (moorit); 1 row white on red (C); repeat in reverse.

The smaller pattern is knitted on the light natural ground as follows:

(1 row plain natural); 2 rows dark brown on white; 2 rows grey on lemon; 1 row red on white (C); repeat in reverse.

The peaks are shaded from bottle-green to medium green, lime green and natural white or very light fawn.

(g) Stocking top from old knickerbocker hose

3 rows medium fawn on moorit; 1 row medium fawn on Shetland black; 2 rows fawn on moorit; 1 row natural white on Shetland black; 1 row natural white on moorit; 1 row grey on natural white (C); repeat in reverse order. The rest of the stocking top is plain dark moorit.

(h) Modern allover jersey in natural colours

5/15/5/5/15/5 repeated. This pattern consists of large Fair-Isle type patterns separated by peerie patterns in sets of two similar patterns of 5 rows each. The medium fawn used is a dyed colour with a pink tone and the grey is almost blue by comparison.

Ribbing: plain moorit; or corrugated rib in moorit with Shetland black/light grey/dark grey/dyed fawn/moorit/natural white (C) sequence repeated in reverse.

(A) First version of 15-row pattern: 1 row of light fawn. 3 rows Shetland black on light fawn; 3 rows moorit on light fawn; 3 rows grey on white (C); 3 rows moorit on light fawn; 3 rows Shetland black on light fawn.

Small patterns: 5 rows each, separated by 2 rows of plain moorit. 2 rows plain moorit; 5 rows light fawn on grey; 2 rows plain moorit; 5 rows natural white on medium fawn; 2 rows plain moorit.

(B) Second version of 15-row pattern: 1 row of plain Shetland black. 3 rows medium fawn on Shetland black; 3 rows grey on Shetland black; 3 rows white on grey (C); 3 rows grey on Shetland black; 3 rows medium fawn on Shetland black.

Small patterns repeated as above but in reverse order. Pattern (A) thus has a grey pattern on each side, while pattern (B) has a fawn version on each side.

(i) Modern allover jersey in natural colours

A very complex modern colour scheme; the pattern sequence is 15/3/9/3/15/3/9/3 repeated. The colour schemes of every second 15-row and 9-row pattern also alternate, so that there are two versions of each. The colours used are Shetland black, moorit, medium (pink) fawn, light fawn, natural white, dark grey, medium grey and a light, almost fawny, grey.

(A) First version of 15-row pattern: 3 rows medium fawn on white; 1 row moorit on white; 2 rows

moorit on light grey; 3 rows Shetland black on light fawn (C); 2 rows moorit on light grey; 1 row moorit on white; 3 rows medium fawn on white. 1 plain white row.

5-row peerie pattern: 1 row plain grey; 3 rows dark grey on light grey; 1 row plain grey.

(B) First version of 9-row pattern: 1 row medium fawn. 2 rows moorit on medium fawn; 1 row moorit on light fawn; 1 row Shetland black on light fawn; 1 row Shetland black on white (C); 1 row Shetland black on light fawn; 1 row moorit on light fawn; 2 rows moorit on medium fawn. 1 row plain medium fawn.

5-row peerie pattern: as above.

(C) Second version of 15-row pattern: 1 row plain white. 3 rows medium grey on white; 1 row dark grey on white; 2 rows dark grey on medium fawn; 1 row moorit on medium fawn; 1 row moorit on white (C); 1 row moorit on medium fawn; 2 rows dark grey on medium fawn; 1 row dark grey on white; 3 rows medium grey on white. 1 row plain white.

5-row peerie pattern: as above.

(D) Second version of 9-row pattern: 1 row medium

grey. 2 rows Shetland black on medium grey; 1 row Shetland black on light grey; 1 row moorit on light grey; 1 row moorit on white (C); 1 row moorit on light grey; 1 row Shetland black on light grey; 2 rows Shetland black on medium grey. 1 row medium grey.

5-row peerie pattern: as above.

(j)   Large star (25 rows)

3 rows medium fawn on white; 3 rows moorit on light fawn; 3 rows dark grey on light fawn; 3 rows black on white; 1 row bright blue on white (or bright red on white) (C); 3 rows black on white; 3 rows dark grey on light fawn; 3 rows moorit on light fawn; 3 rows medium fawn on white.

(k)   15-row pattern alternating with 4-row peerie pattern

Large pattern: 2 rows medium grey on white; 2 rows medium blue on white; 3 rows light blue on white; 1 row dark red on white (C); 3 rows light blue on white; 2 rows medium blue on white; 2 rows medium grey on white. 1 row white to separate patterns.

Small pattern: 4 rows blue on white.

PART THREE

PATTERNS

The Pattern Notebook

Contents

The size of the patterns is marked at the bottom of the pages, e.g. **(15)**. Allover patterns are marked **(AO)**, etc.

One space in a chart represents one stitch in a row of knitting. The black dots represent the pattern colour in use in any row and the white squares represent the background colour. This does not necessarily suggest the use of a dark pattern colour on a light ground. All of these patterns can equally well be knitted in light pattern colours on a dark ground.

There is no indication of horizontal size, i.e., the number of stitches along the row in any one complete repeat of a pattern. For the larger patterns such as the large stars this is almost always the same as their size in rows – most 25-row stars are also 25 stitches wide. The smaller patterns are very adaptable in width according to the size of joining cross or other pattern used, and the horixontal repeat can be altered to a convenient size by varying the cross used. A selection is given on page 68 in 11-row, 13-row and 19-row sizes. These can be adapted to other sizes and examples will be found in all the sections of complete patterns with a variety of joining devices.

Certain pages (90, 91, 98, 100, 105, 106, 108, 109, 110, 111, 115 and 117) do not show complete patterns for reasons of space, but show instead collections of isolated motifs. From these, complete border patterns can be made up on your own graph paper by linking them along the row by suitable crosses or smaller patterns. It is best to leave no more than 7 stitches in one colour, to avoid long loops on the reverse of the work, and new arrangements must allow for this. With the larger patterns the same cross is usually used for each motif (see pp. 103 and 112).

To find the horizontal repeat, or span, of a pattern, count along a row in the chart from any stitch to the stitch before the first counted. The patterns given are not necessarily shown in complete repeats.

Few of these patterns have names beyond those that are largely self-evident: Blocks, Kilt or Flag, Tree of Life or Fern, Anchor, Hearts, Wreath, Skull and Crossbones, Flower, Spider, Waves and H's. More romantic names are a recent invention.

Peerie patterns: alternate with larger border patterns to make up allover patterns. Use as edging for star panels in jerseys (knitted vertically), yokes, etc. Effective with thick yarn.

Border patterns: used to make up allover patterns and to decorate smaller items such as stocking tops, glove cuffs, ski caps, etc. Faith, Hope and Charity (p. 95) from an old Sandwick scarf.

Fair Isle patterns: are often knitted in two ways – (see p. 108 for examples of both) – surrounded by a frame in the same colour or inside a lozenge of contrasting colour. This second method is correct (in that it is the old Fair Isle method). The confusion has arisen from the difficulty in showing this on a chart.

Large stars and seeding: often used together in so-called Norwegian work in men's jerseys.

Allover patterns: very many more exist than are shown here. Many adaptations from these basic ideas can be worked out for different sizes. The motifs on pp. 132 and 134 may be used to decorate diced patterns for scarves, pullovers, etc.

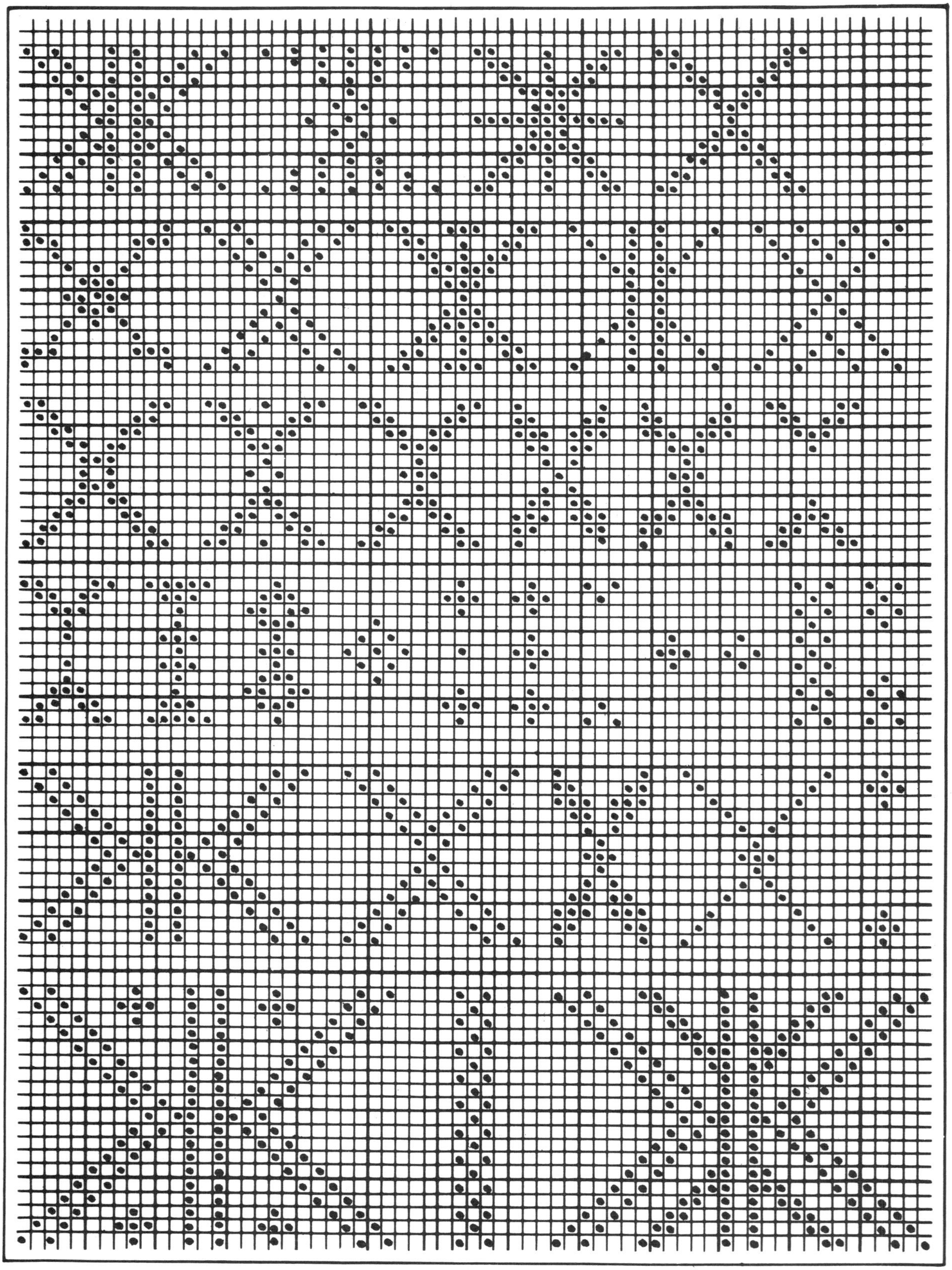

(1, 2, 3)

(3, 4)

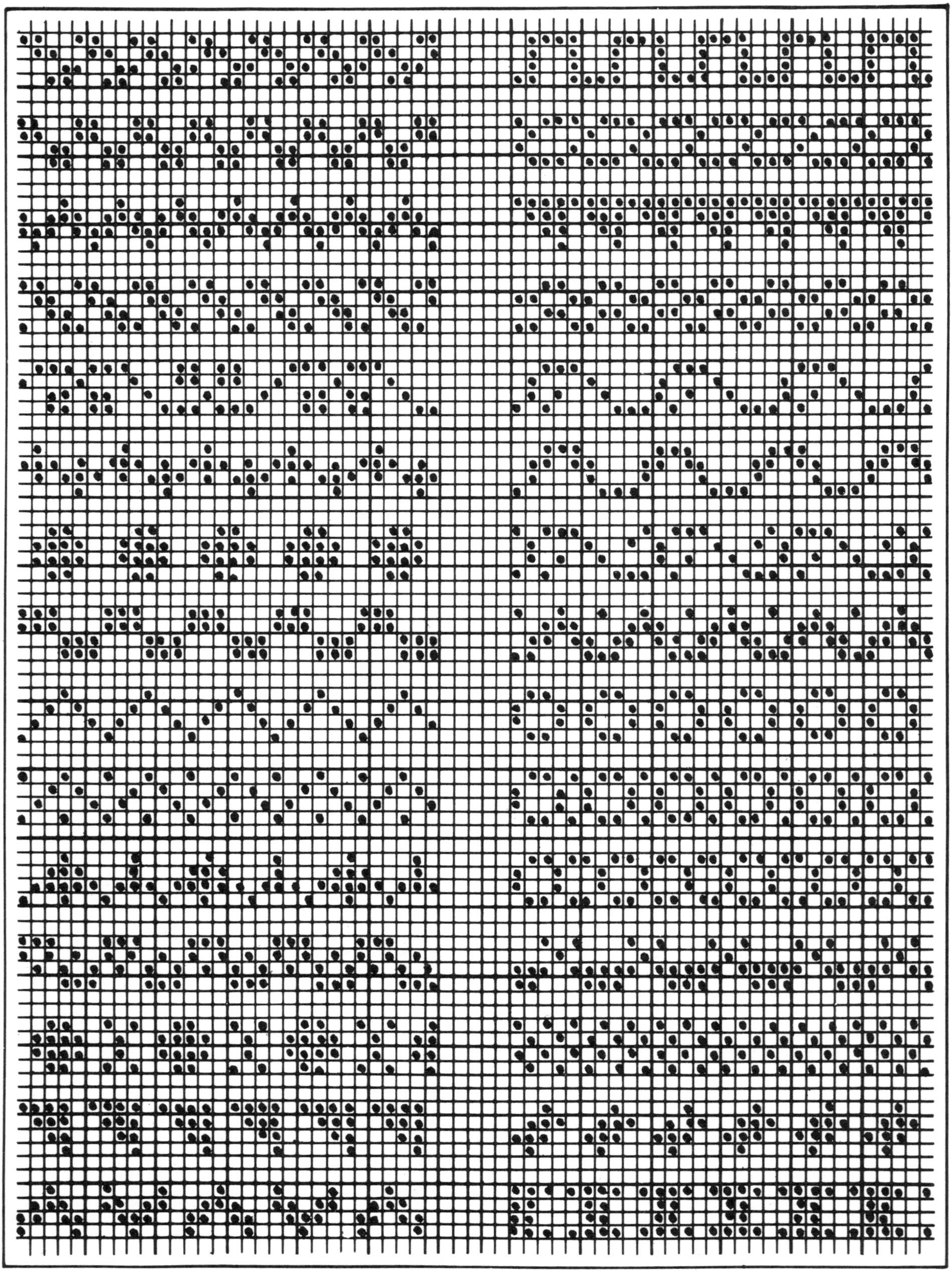

(4)

Close-up of jersey knitted in Fair Isle in 1895 (Shetland Museum)

Front panel from jersey knitted in Fair Isle, bought in Thurso in 1919 (NMAS)

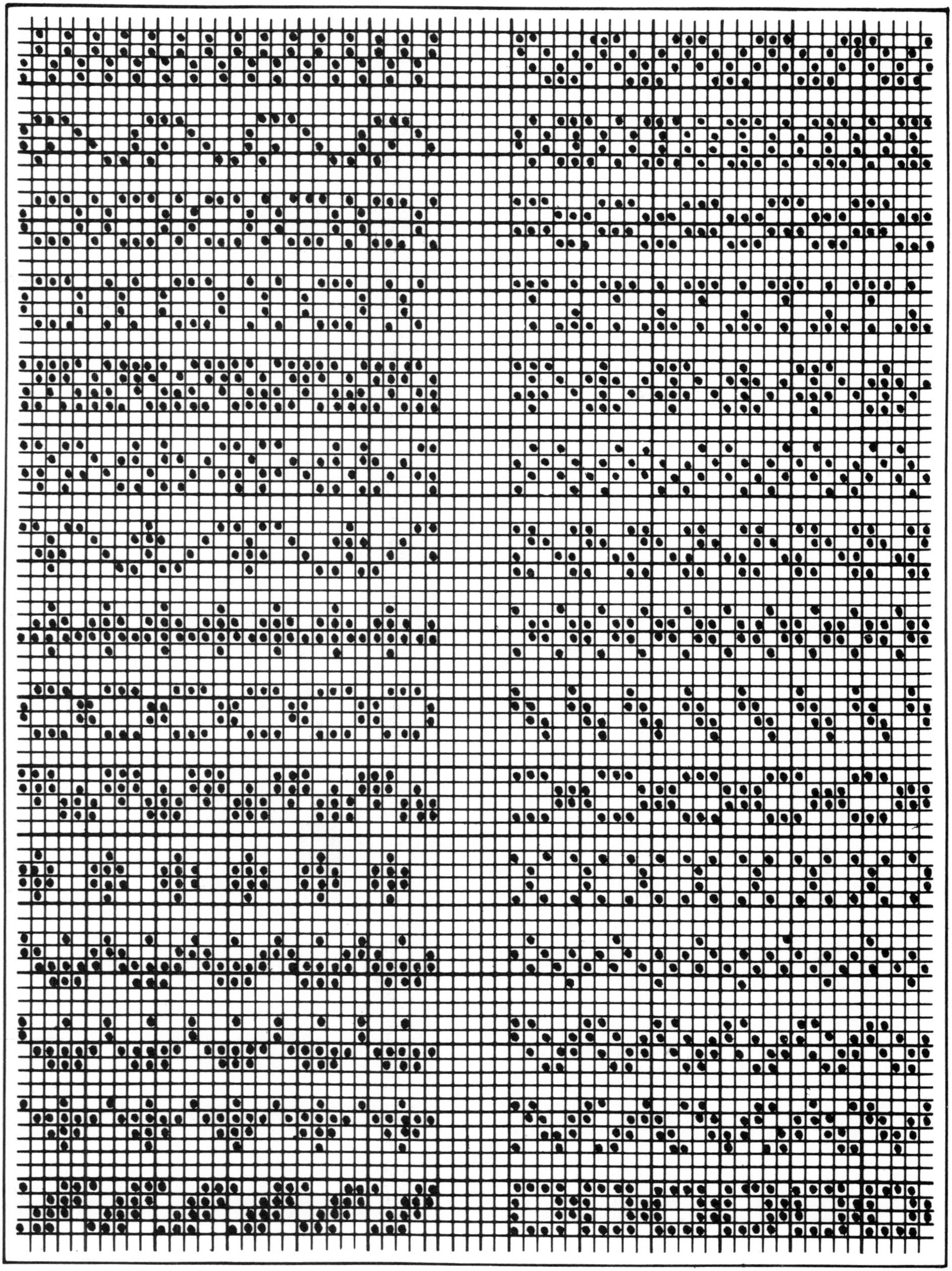

(4)

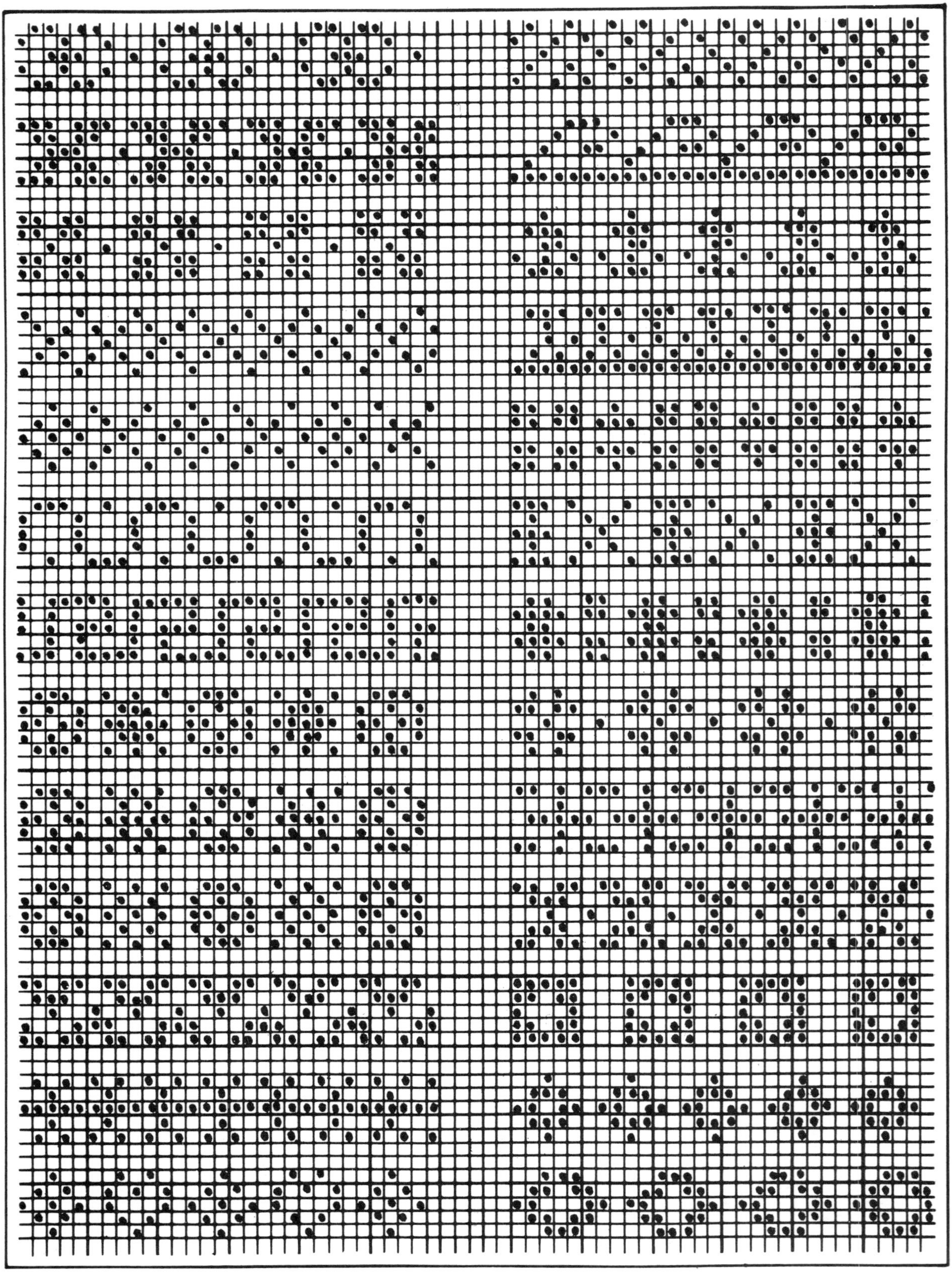

(5)

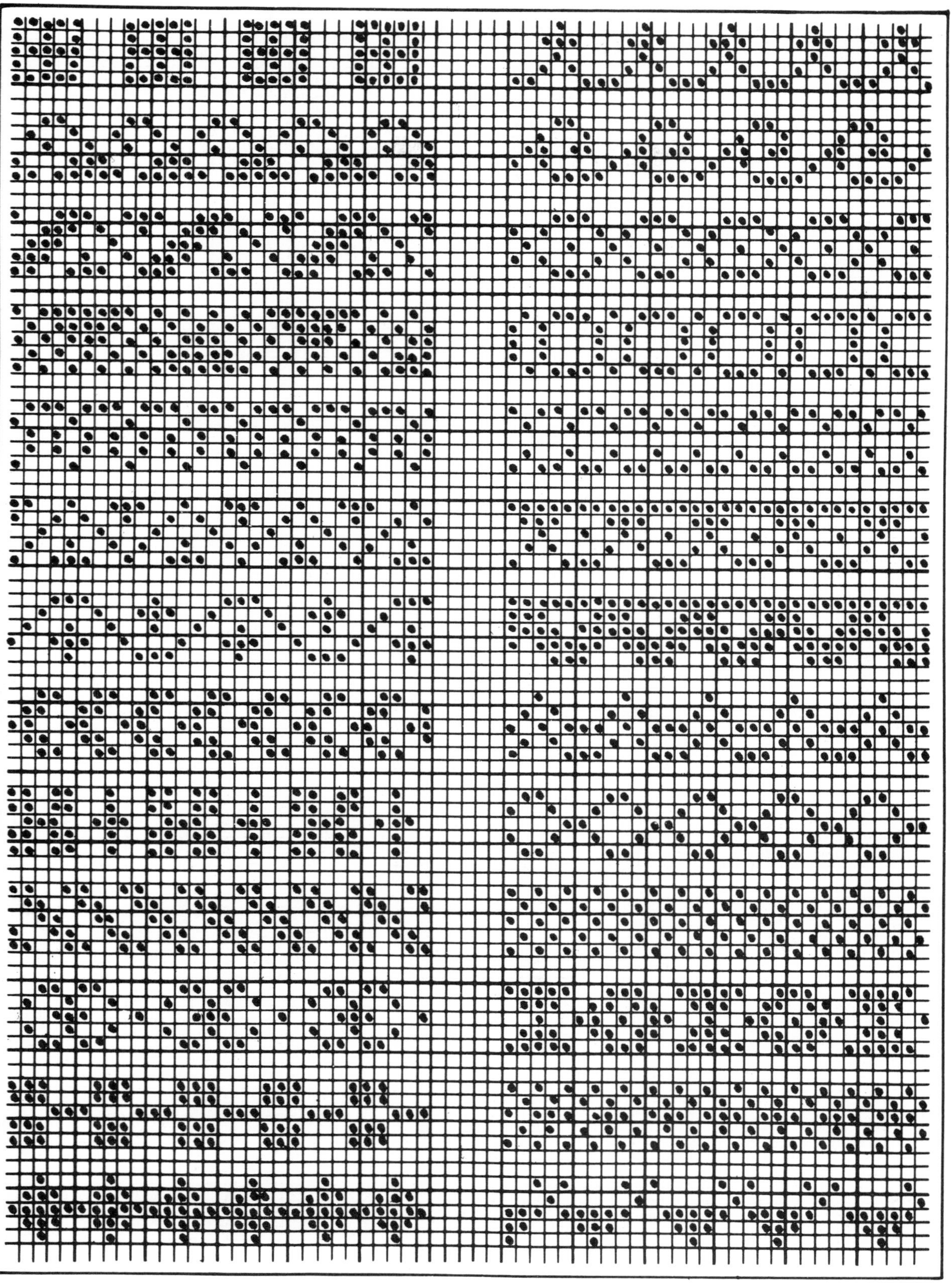

(5)

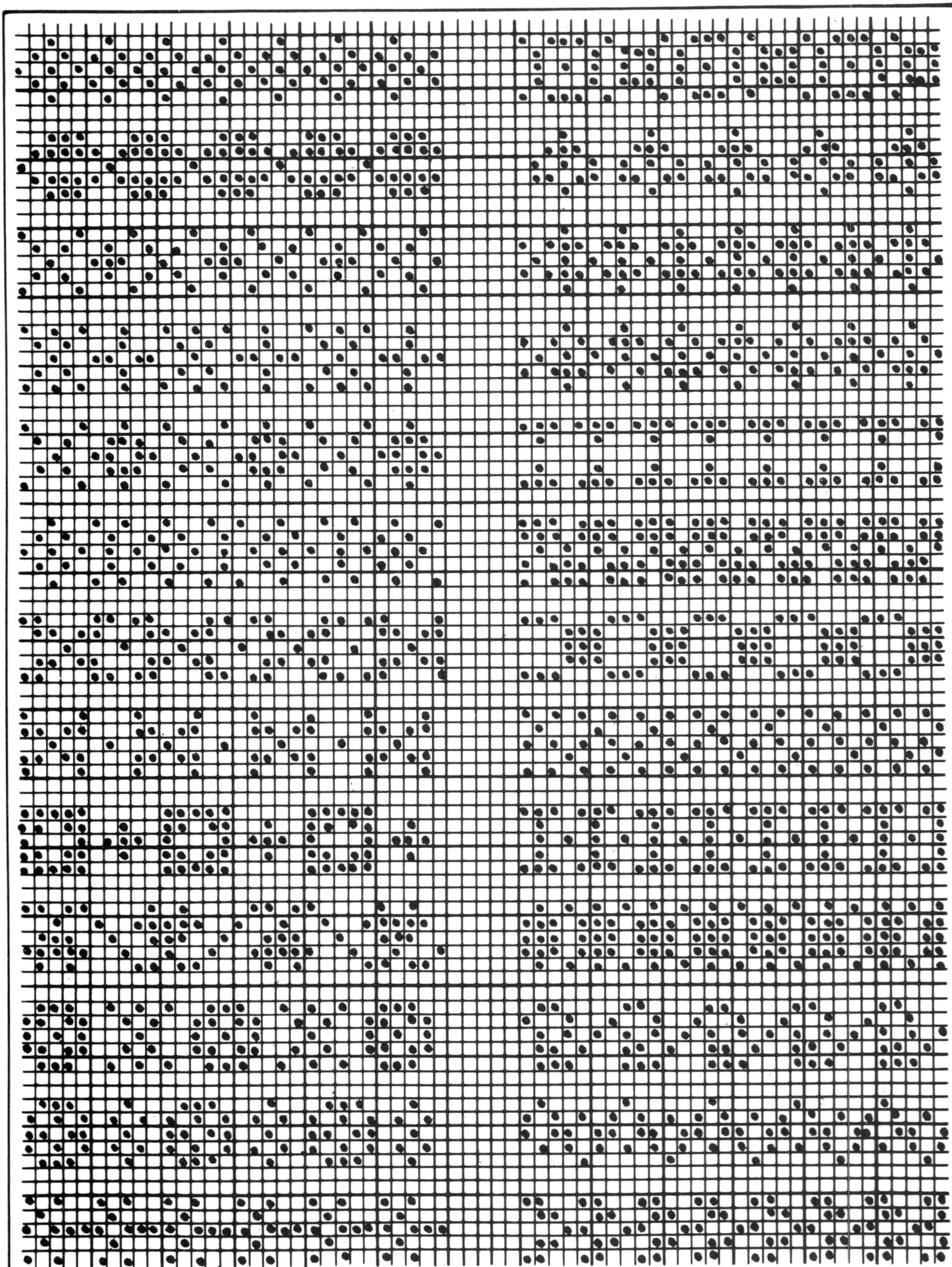

(5)

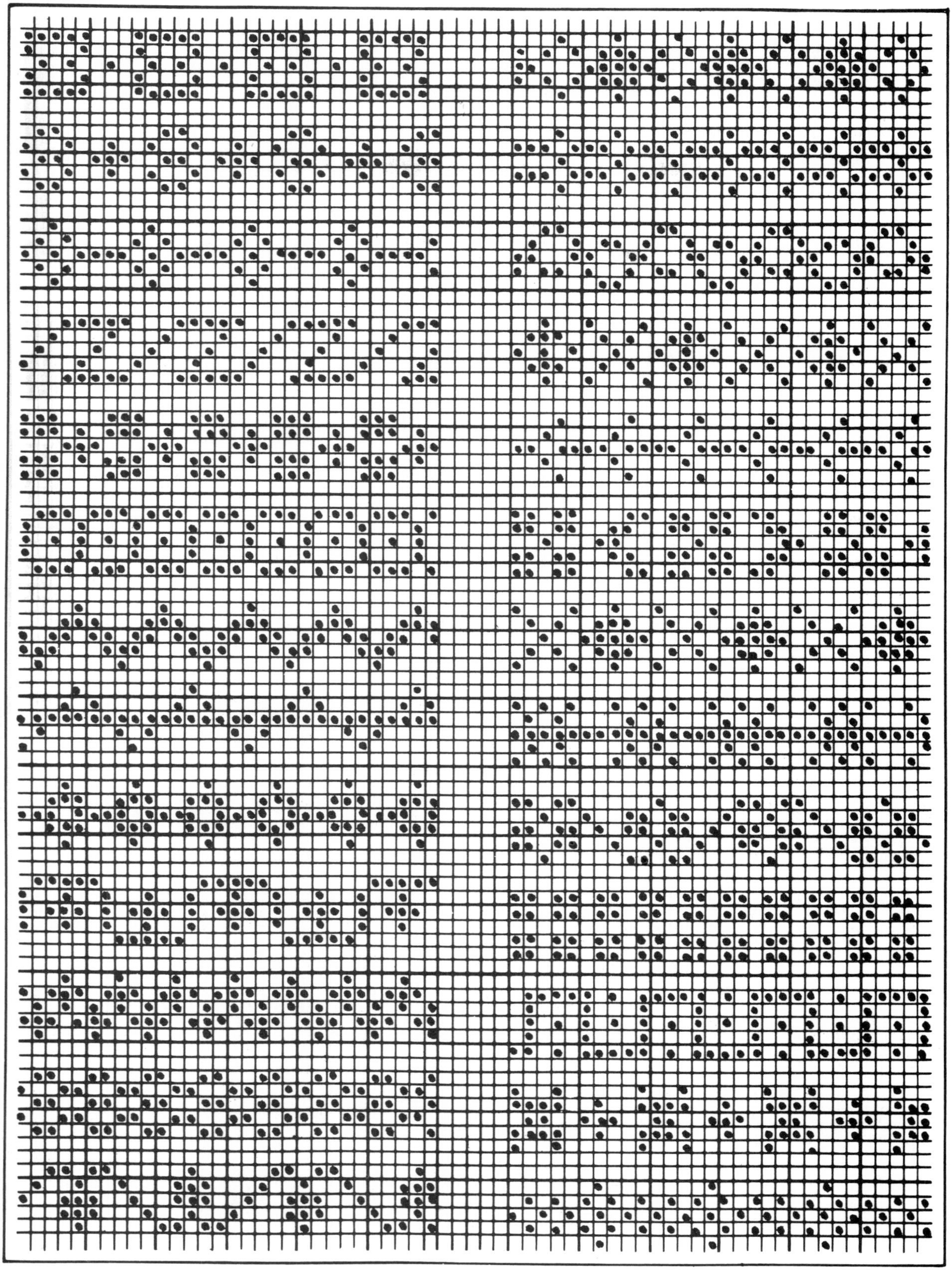

(5)

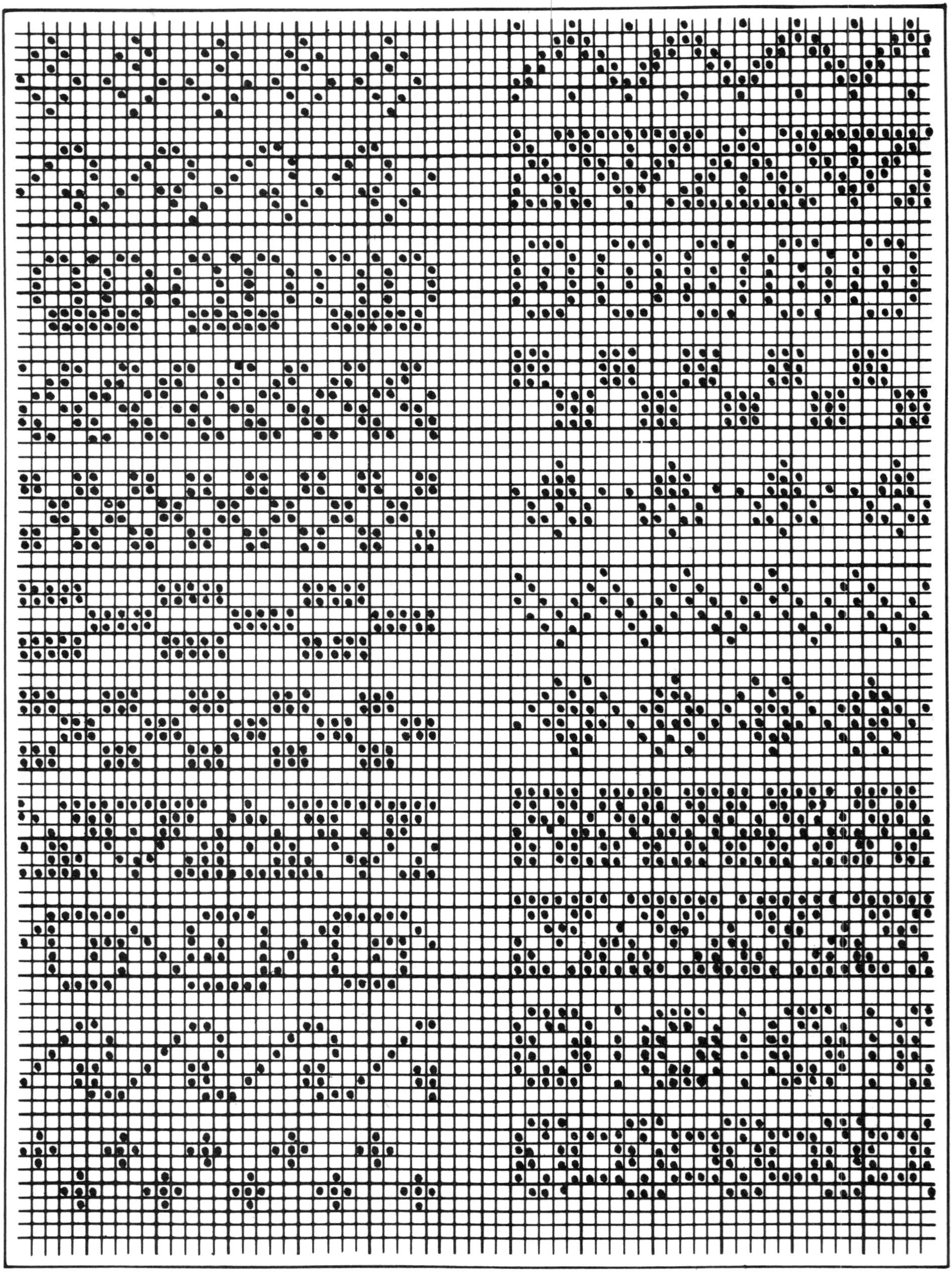

(**6**)

(6, 7)

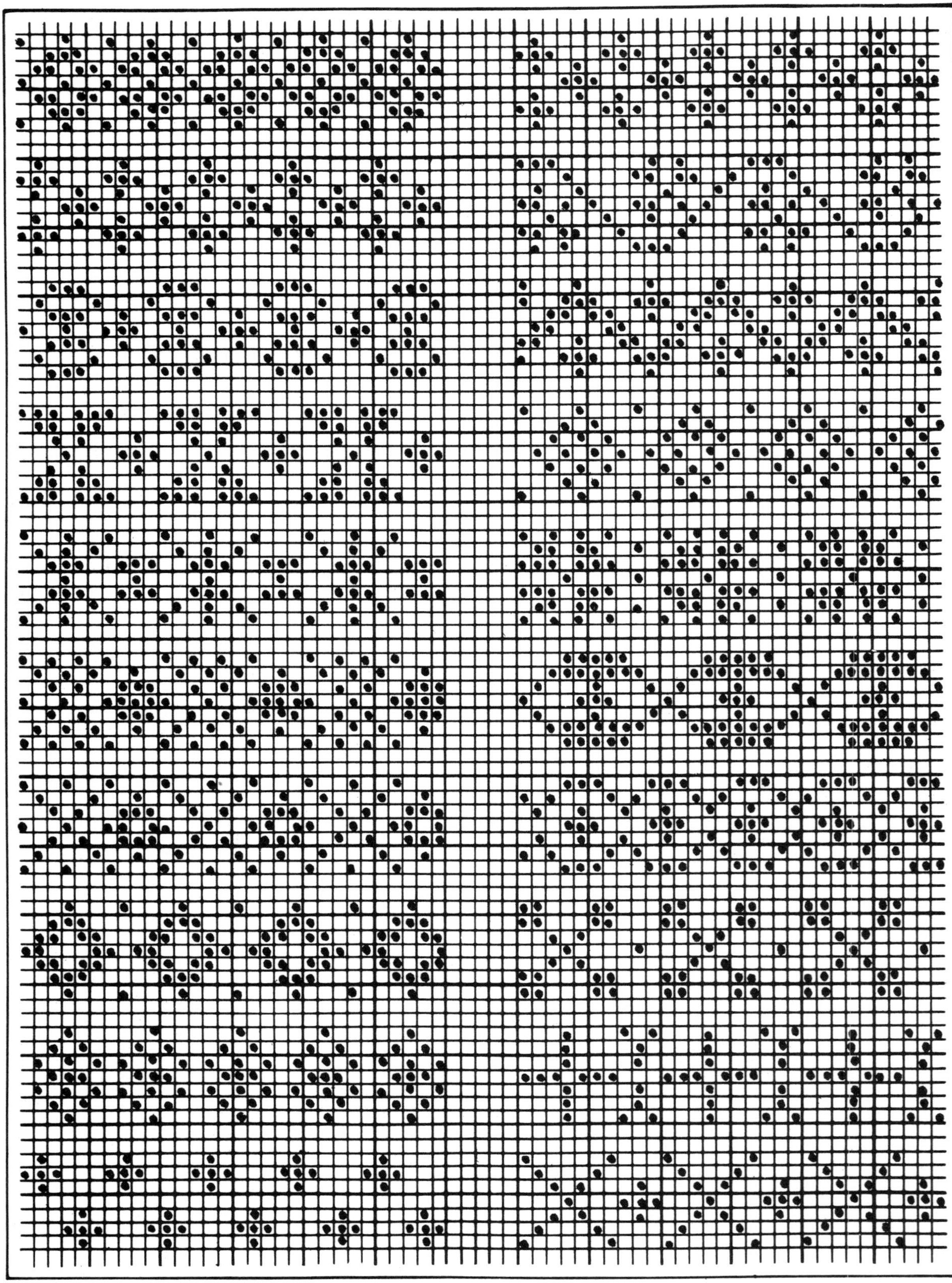

(7)

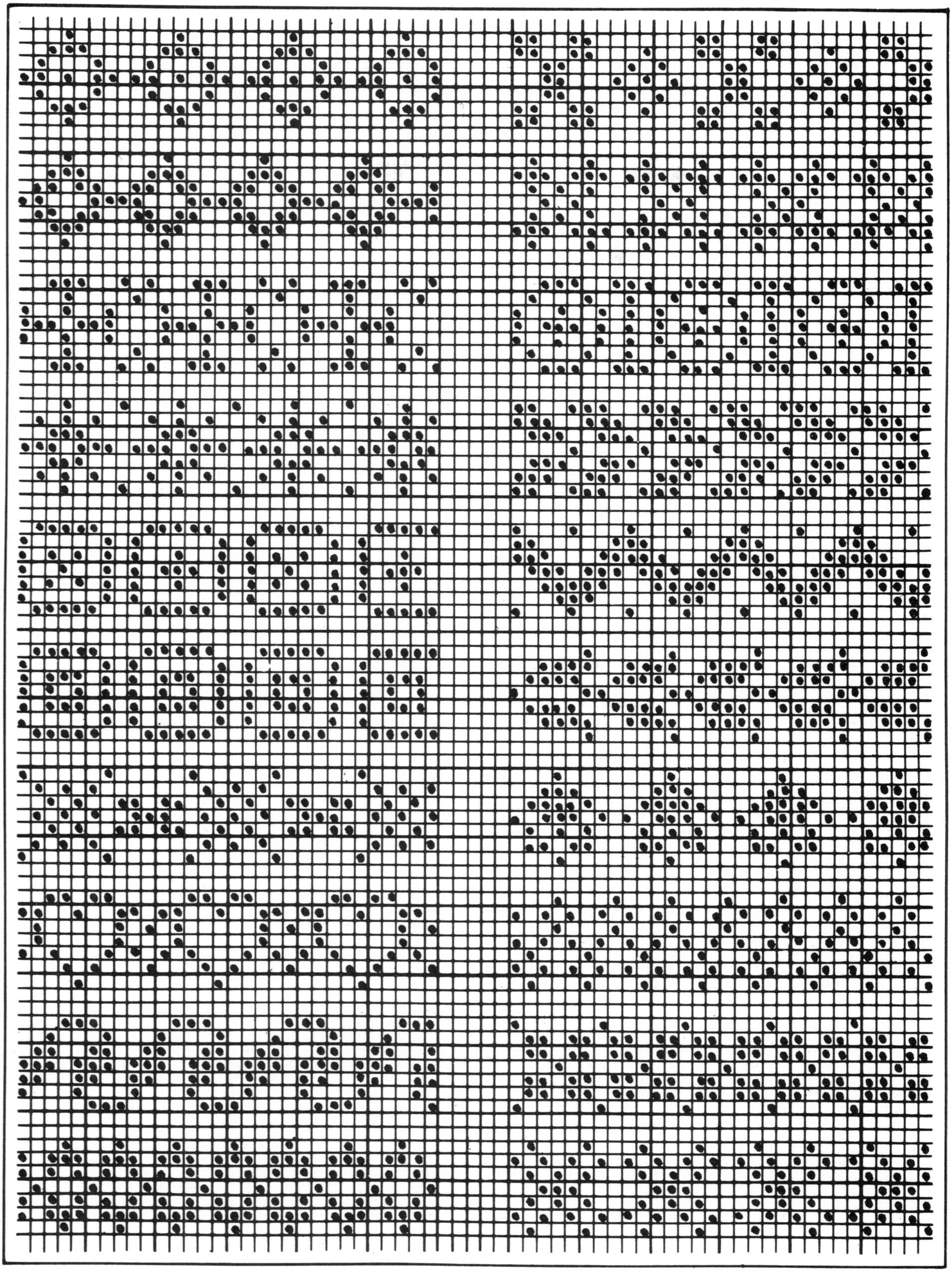

(7)

82

(9)

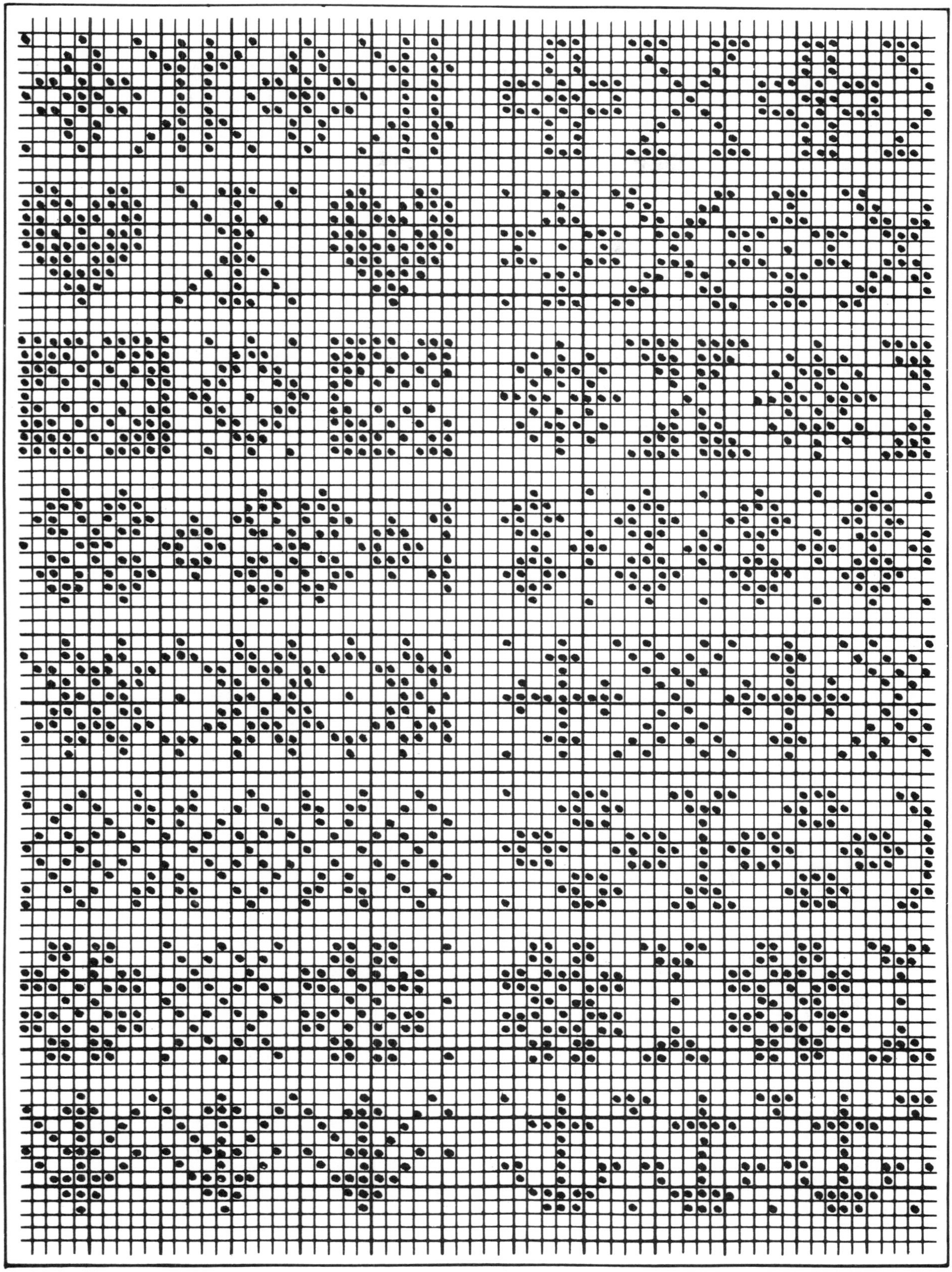

(9)

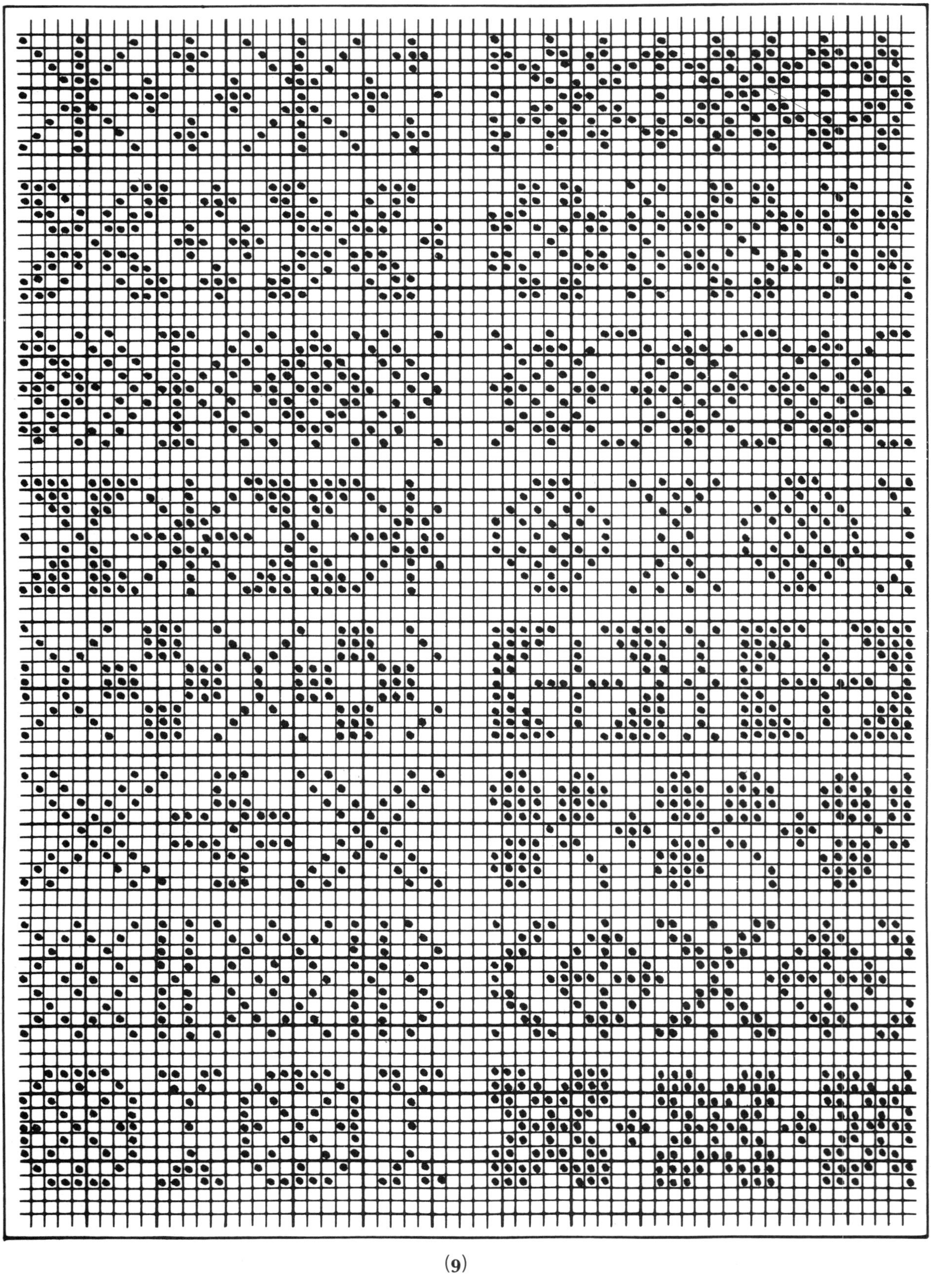

(9)

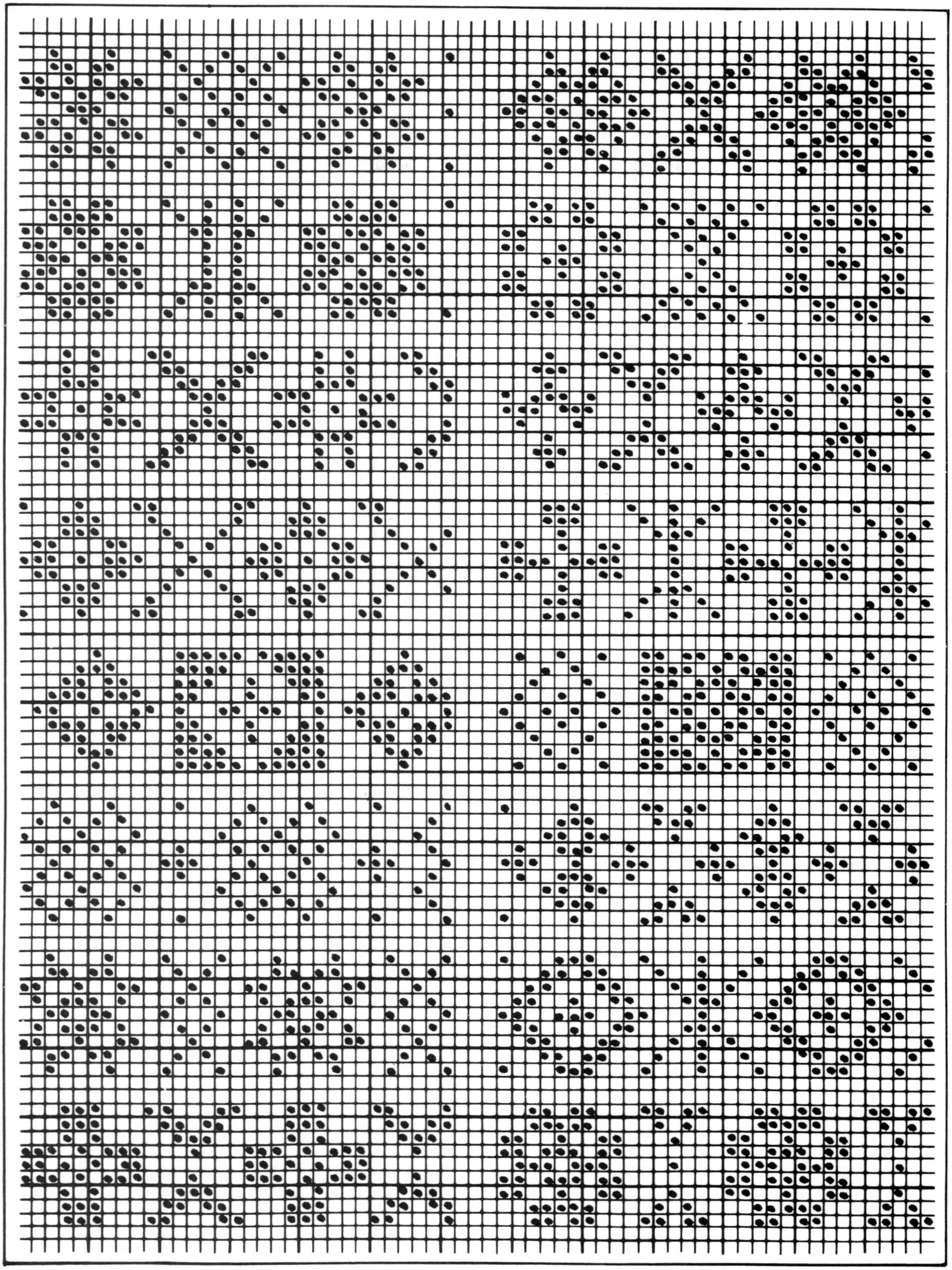

(9)

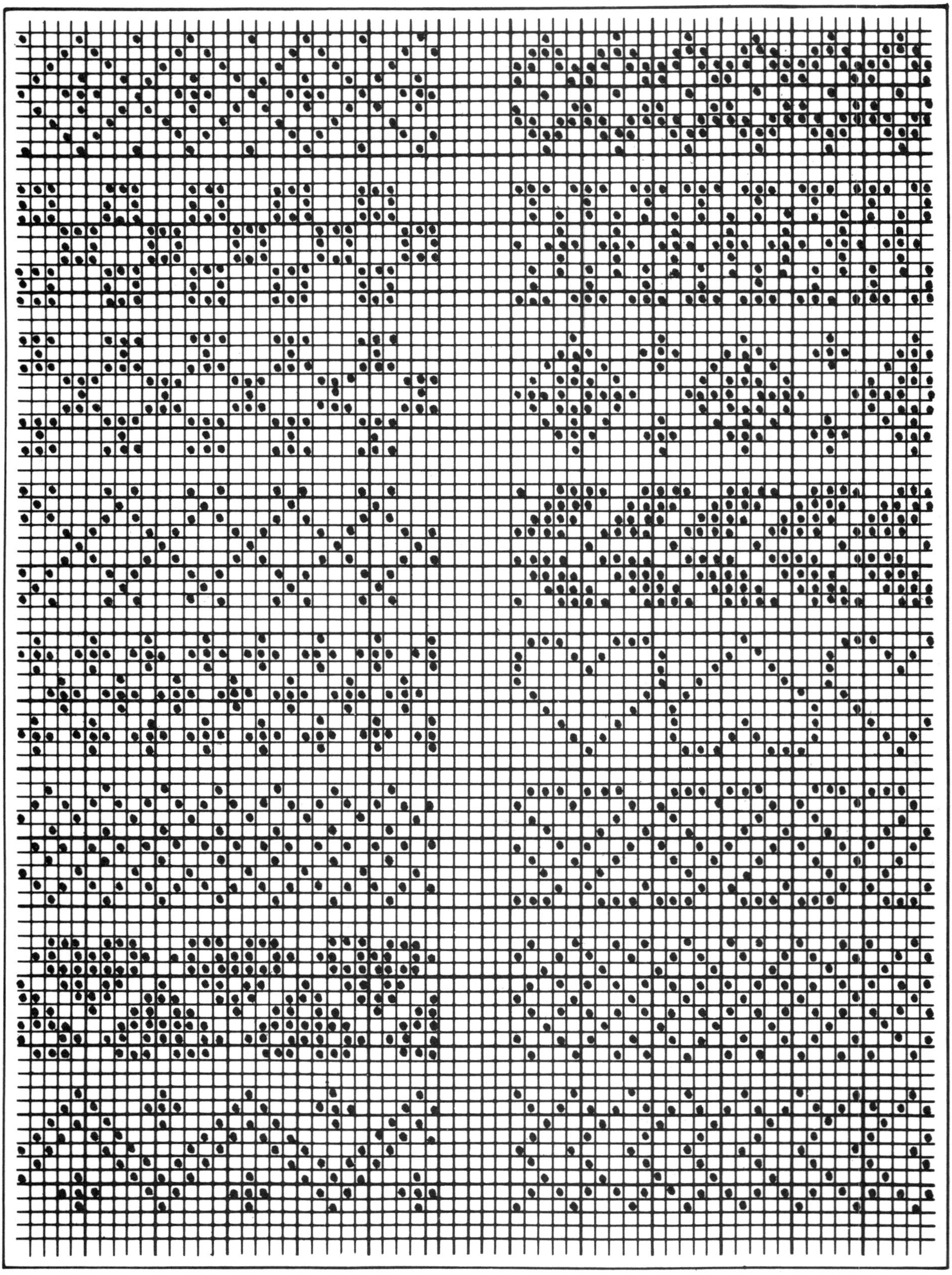

(9)

(8, 10)

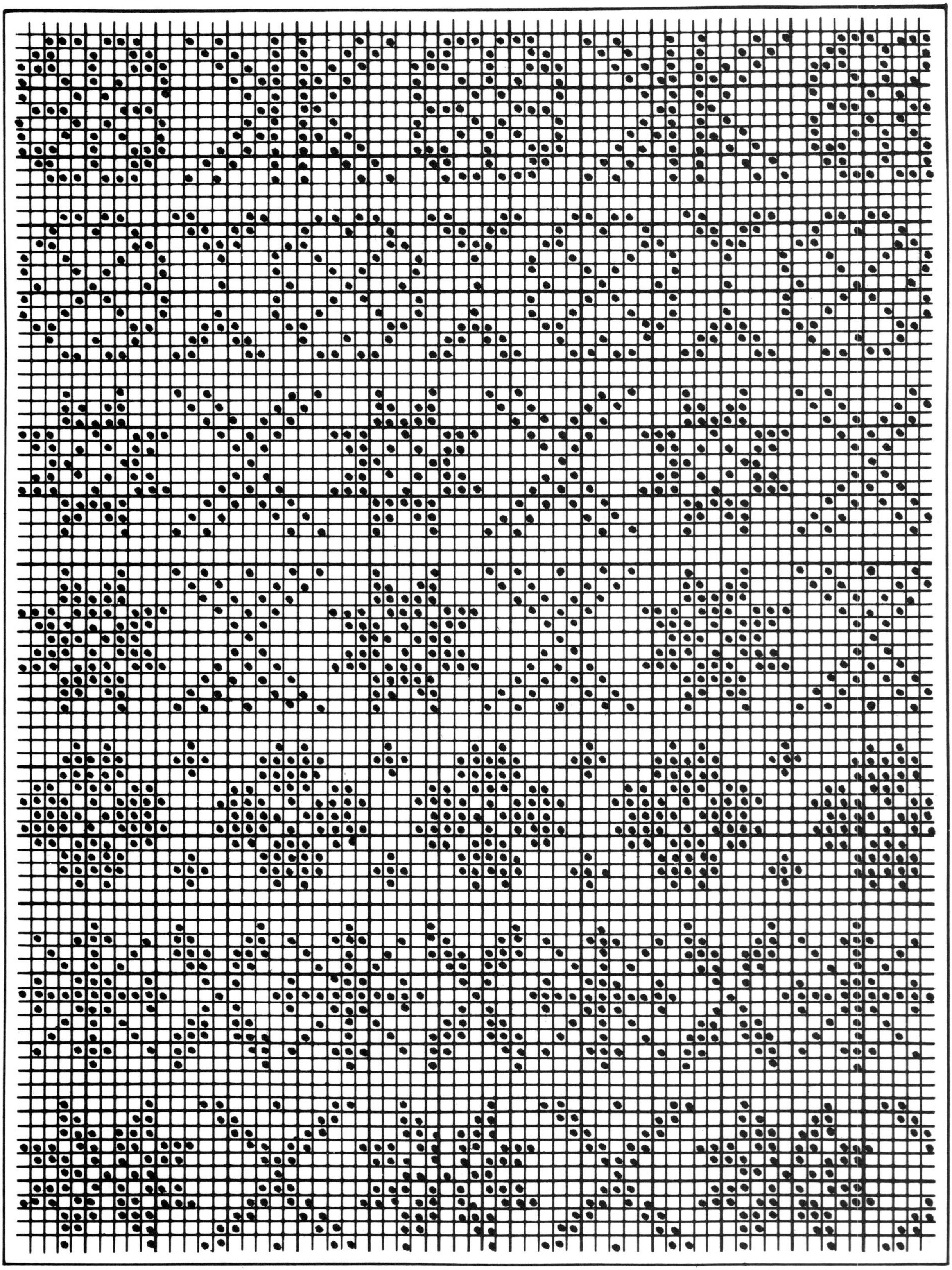

(11)

(11)

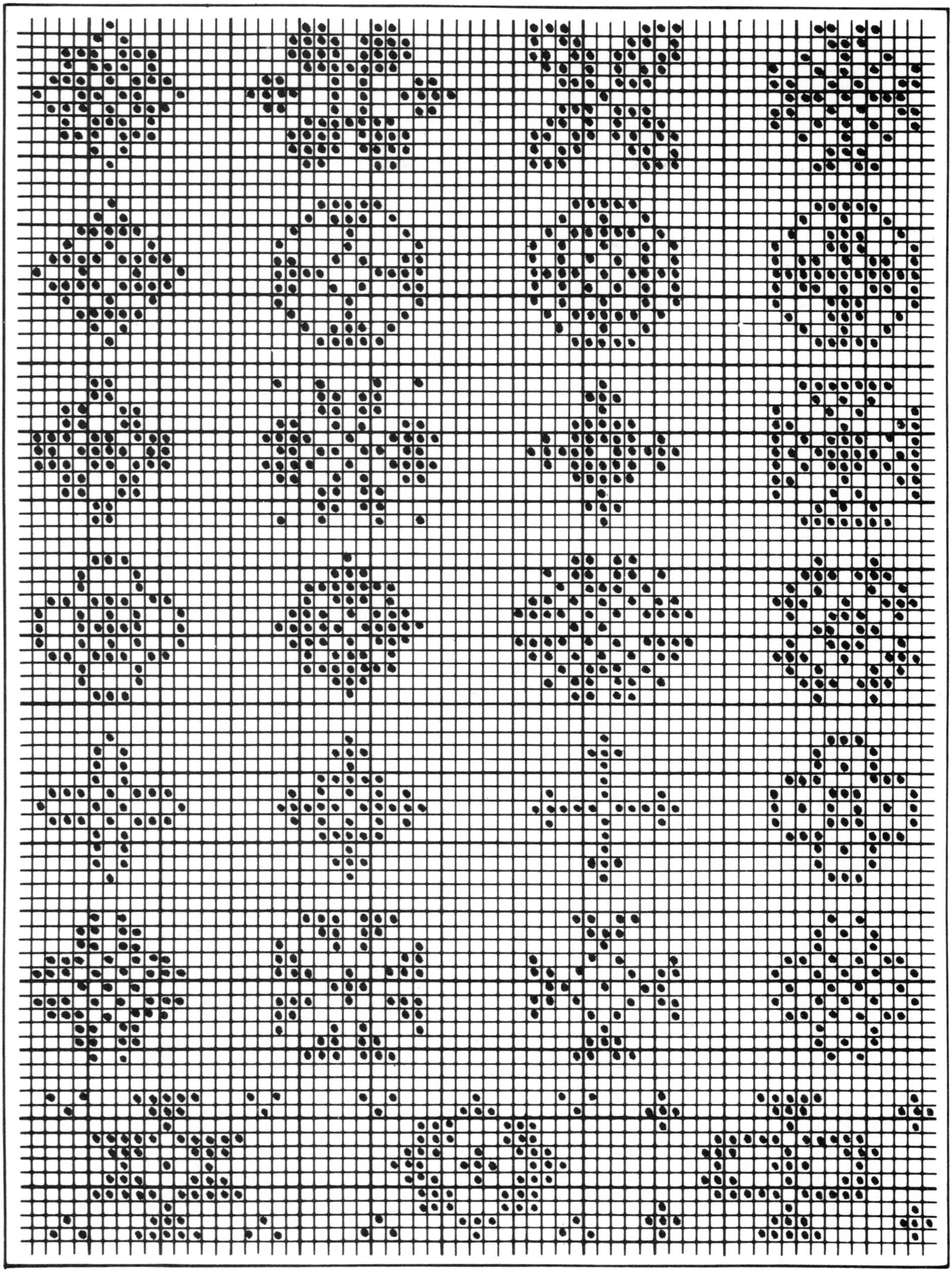

(11)

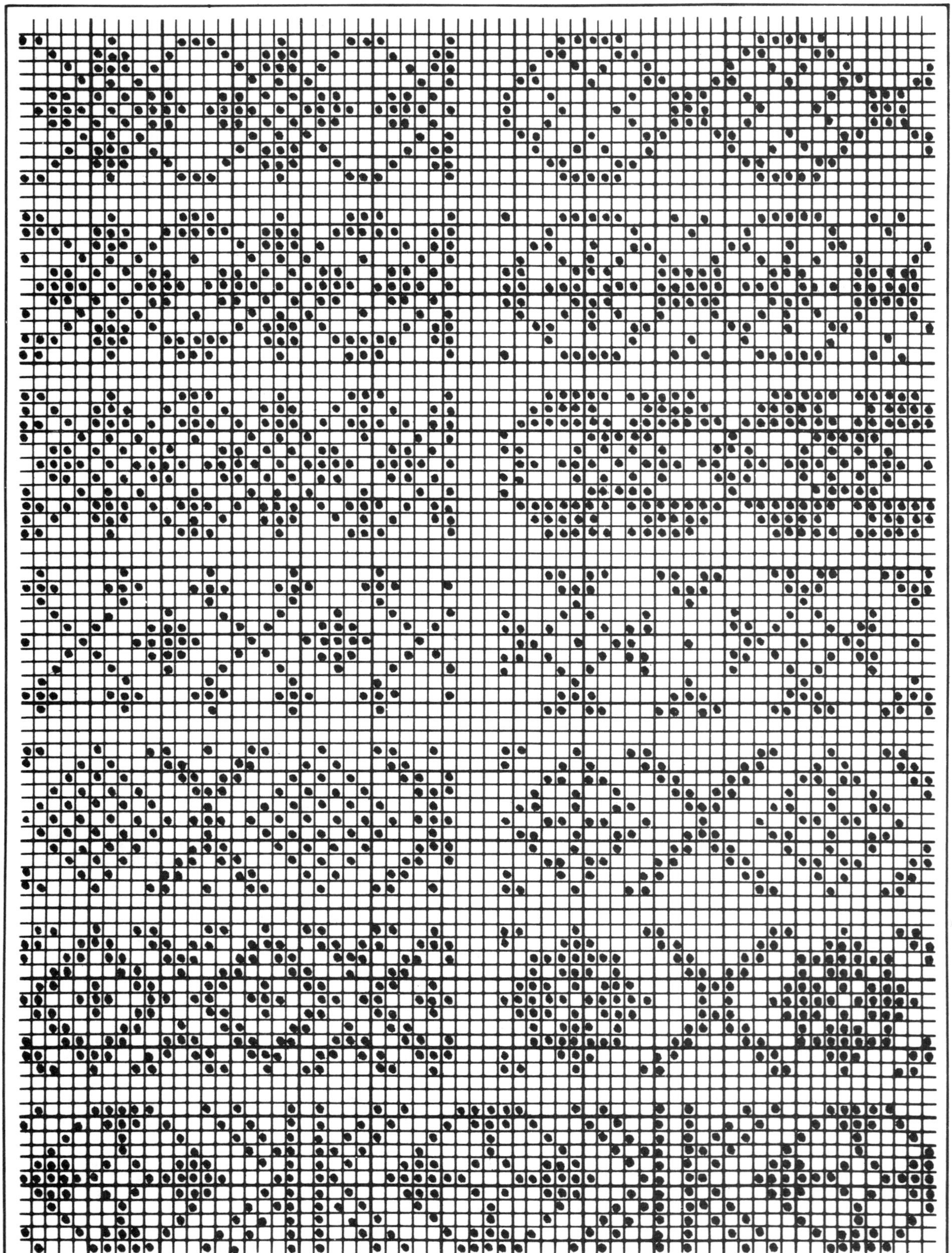

(11)

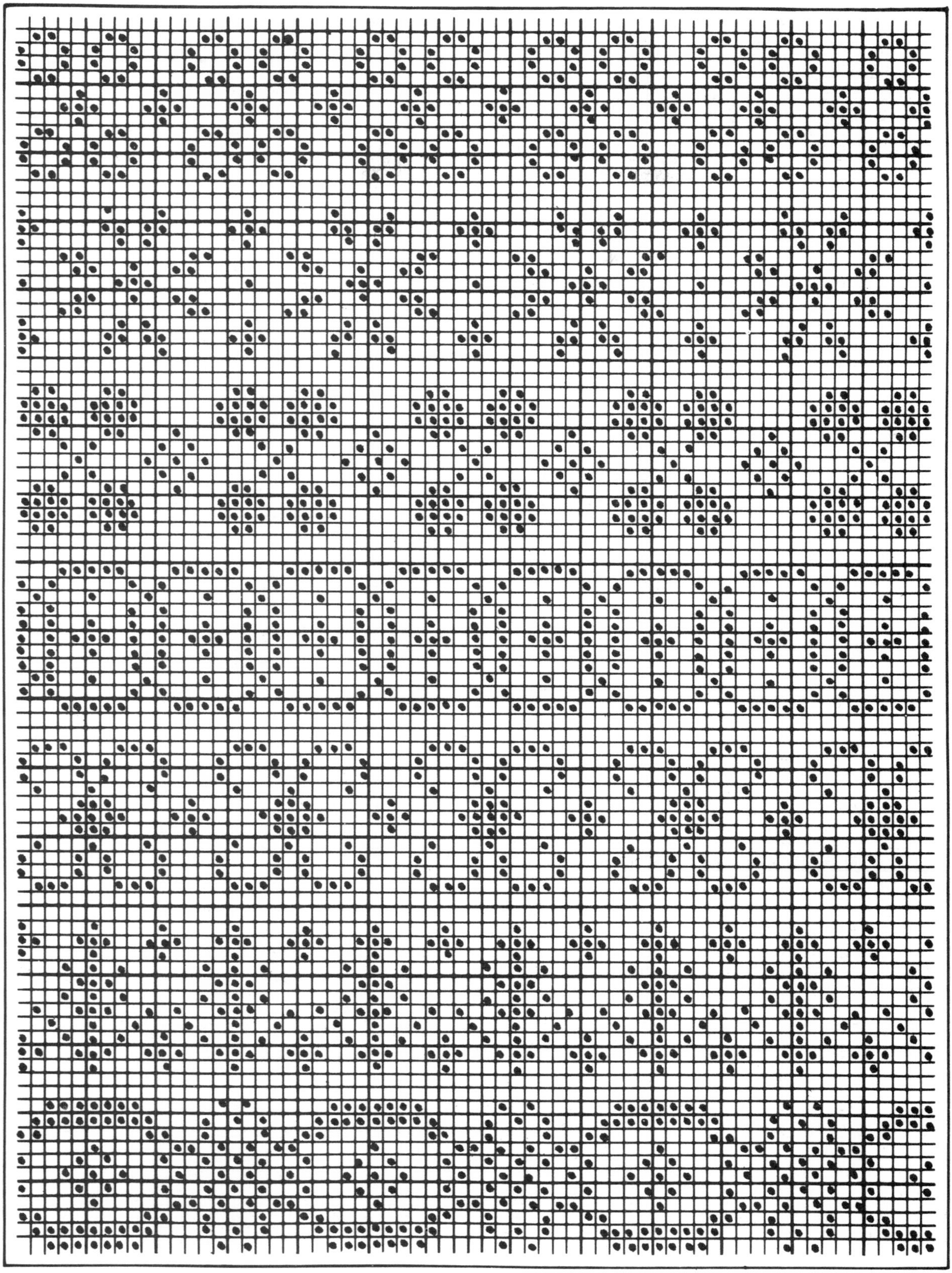

(11)

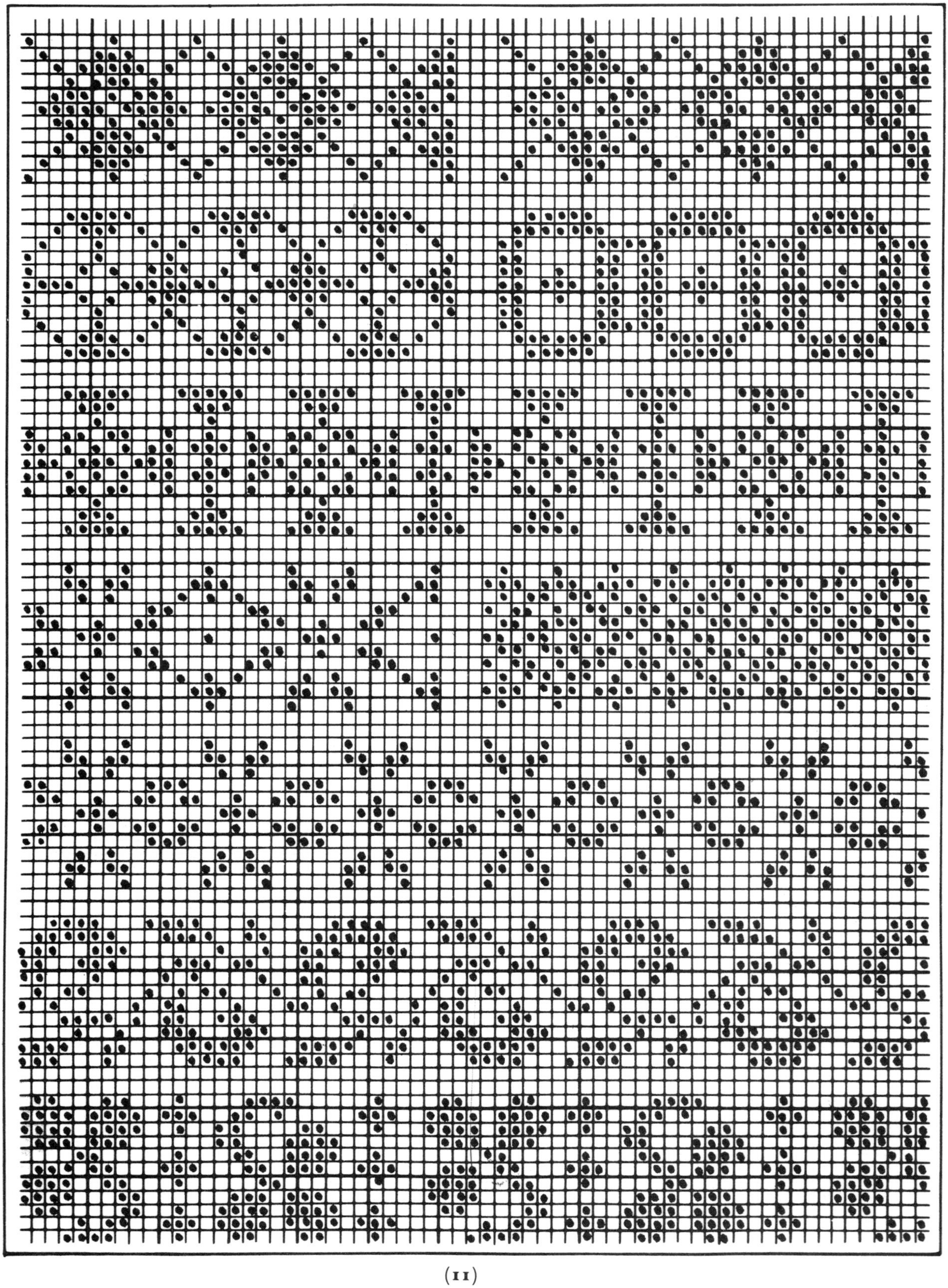

(11)

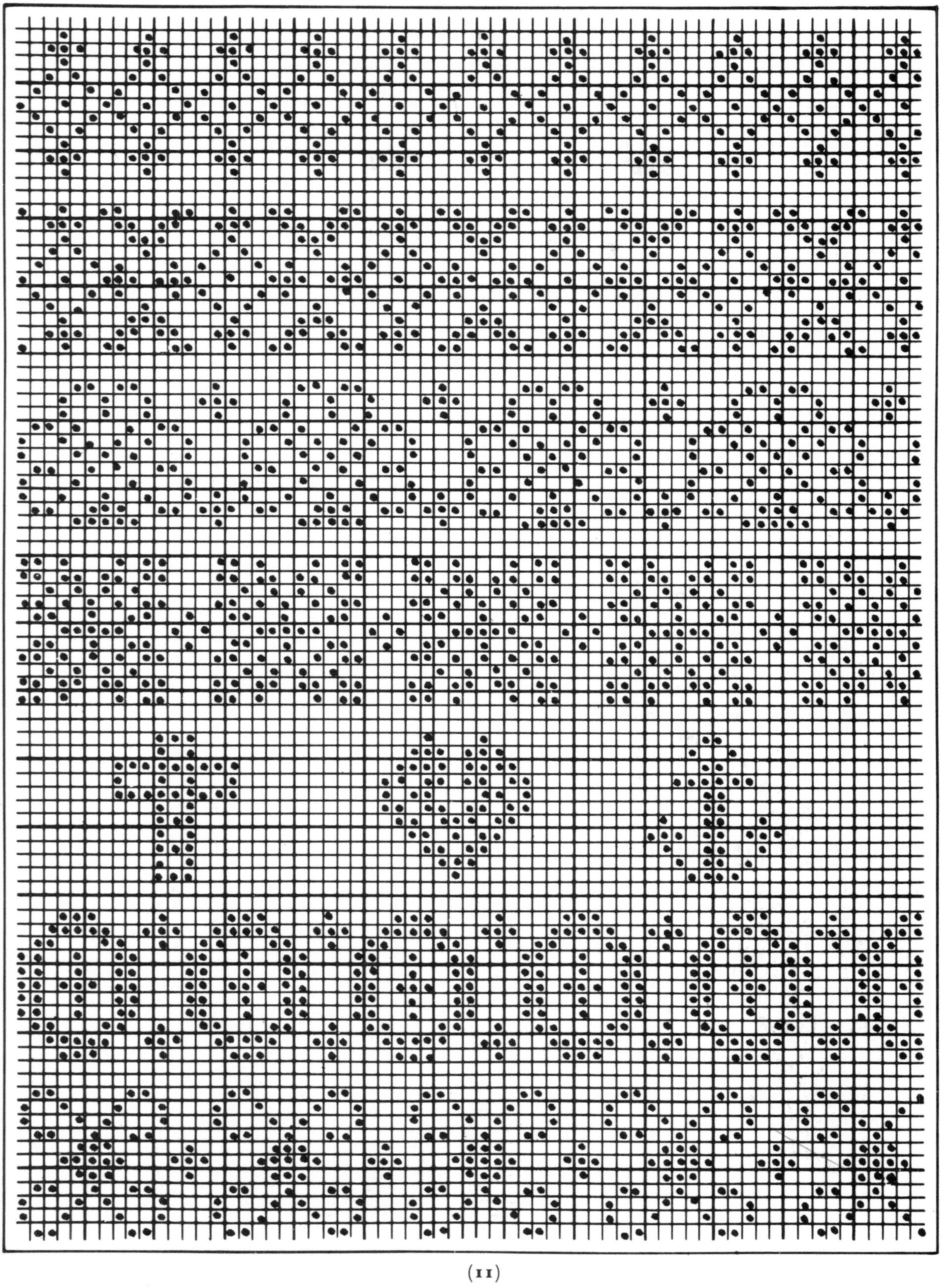

(11)

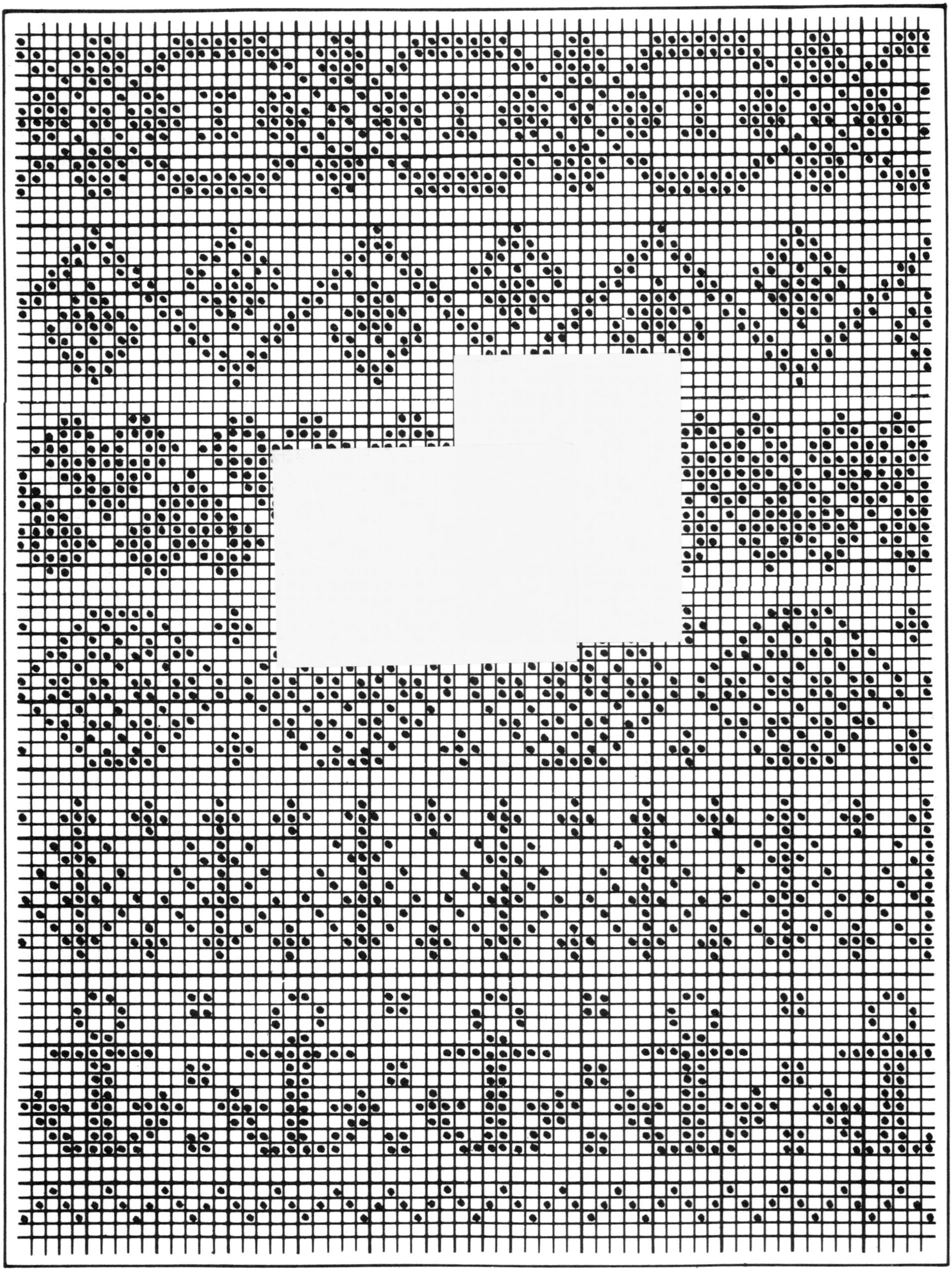

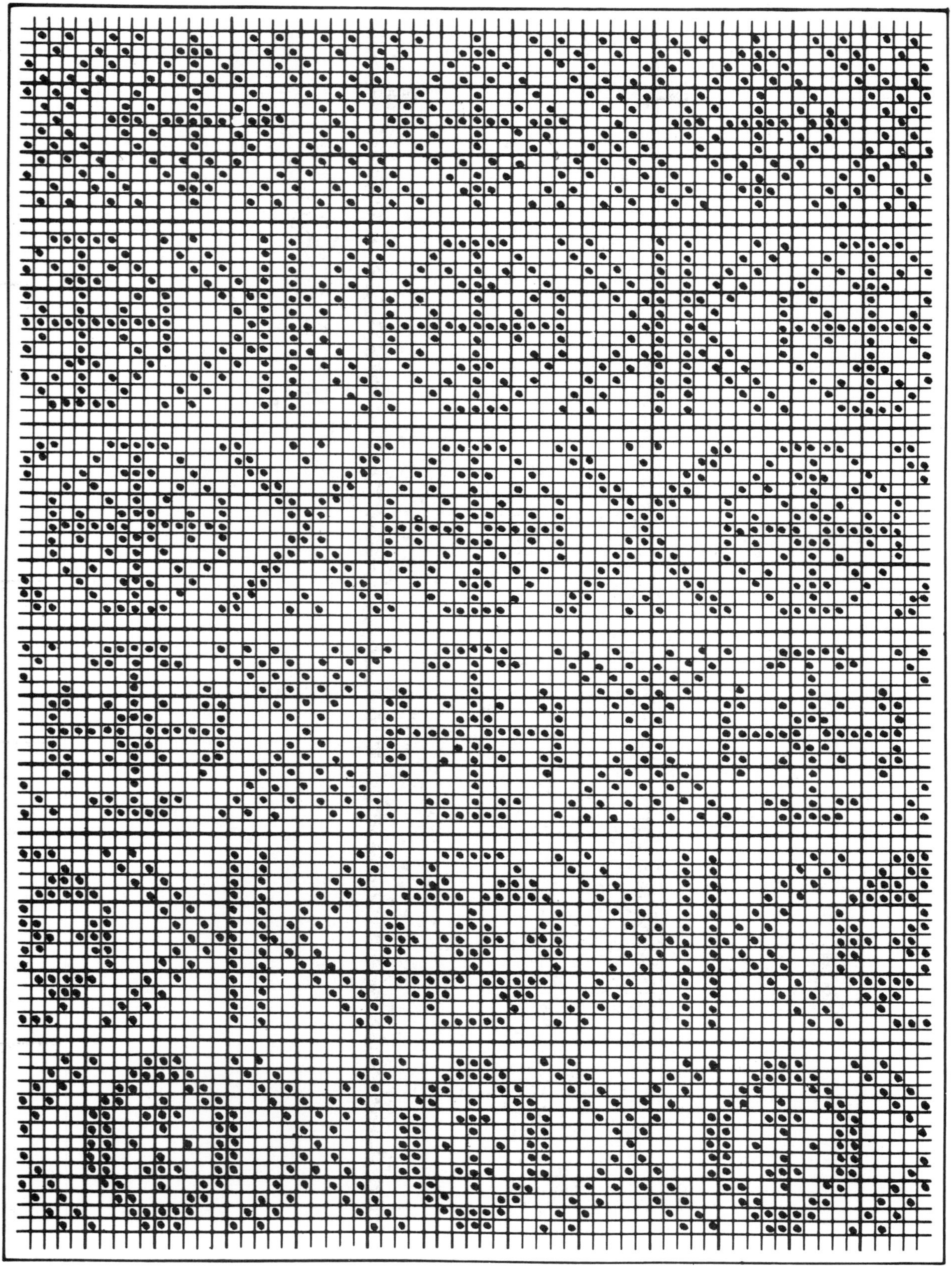

(13)

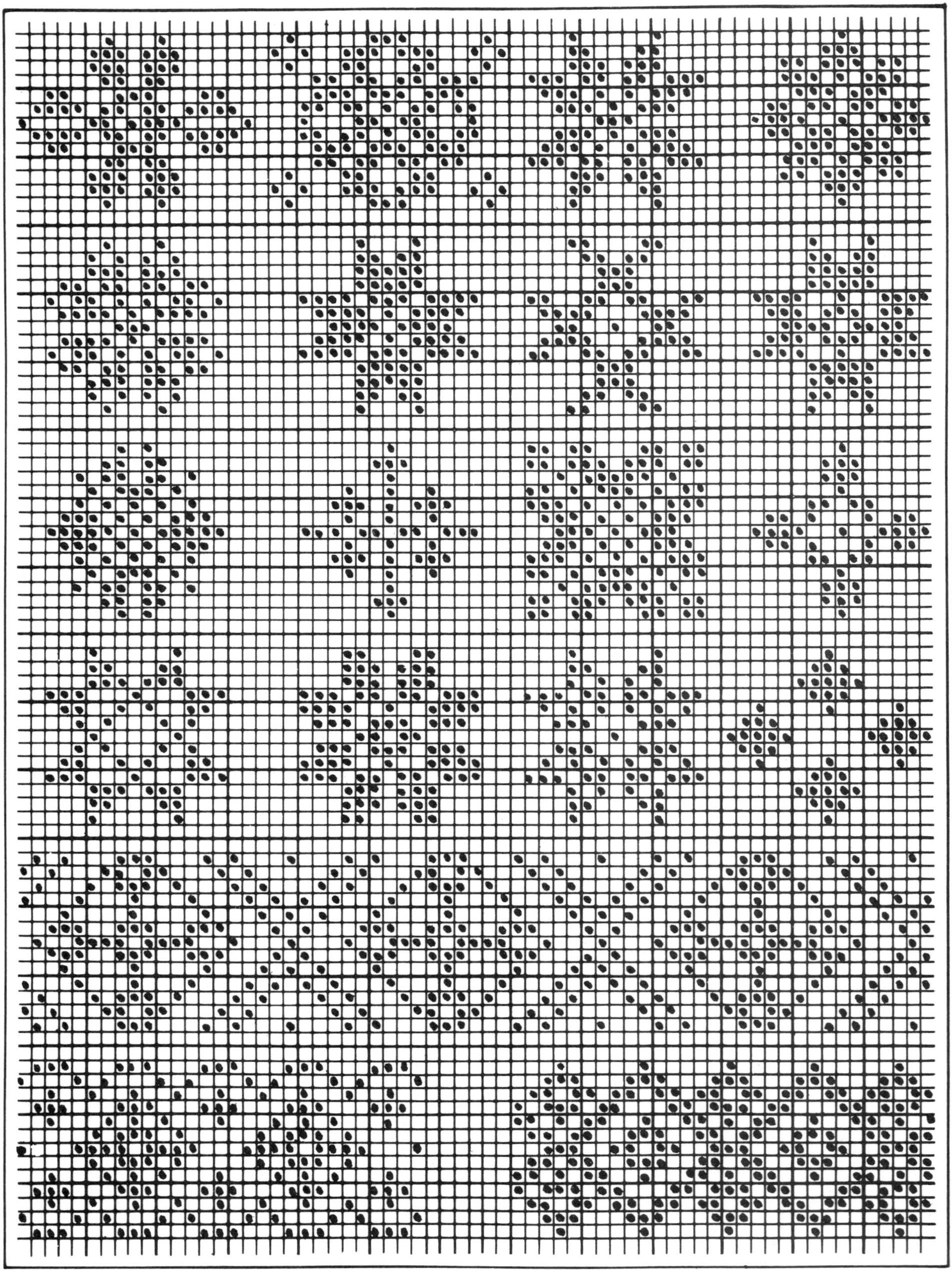

(13)

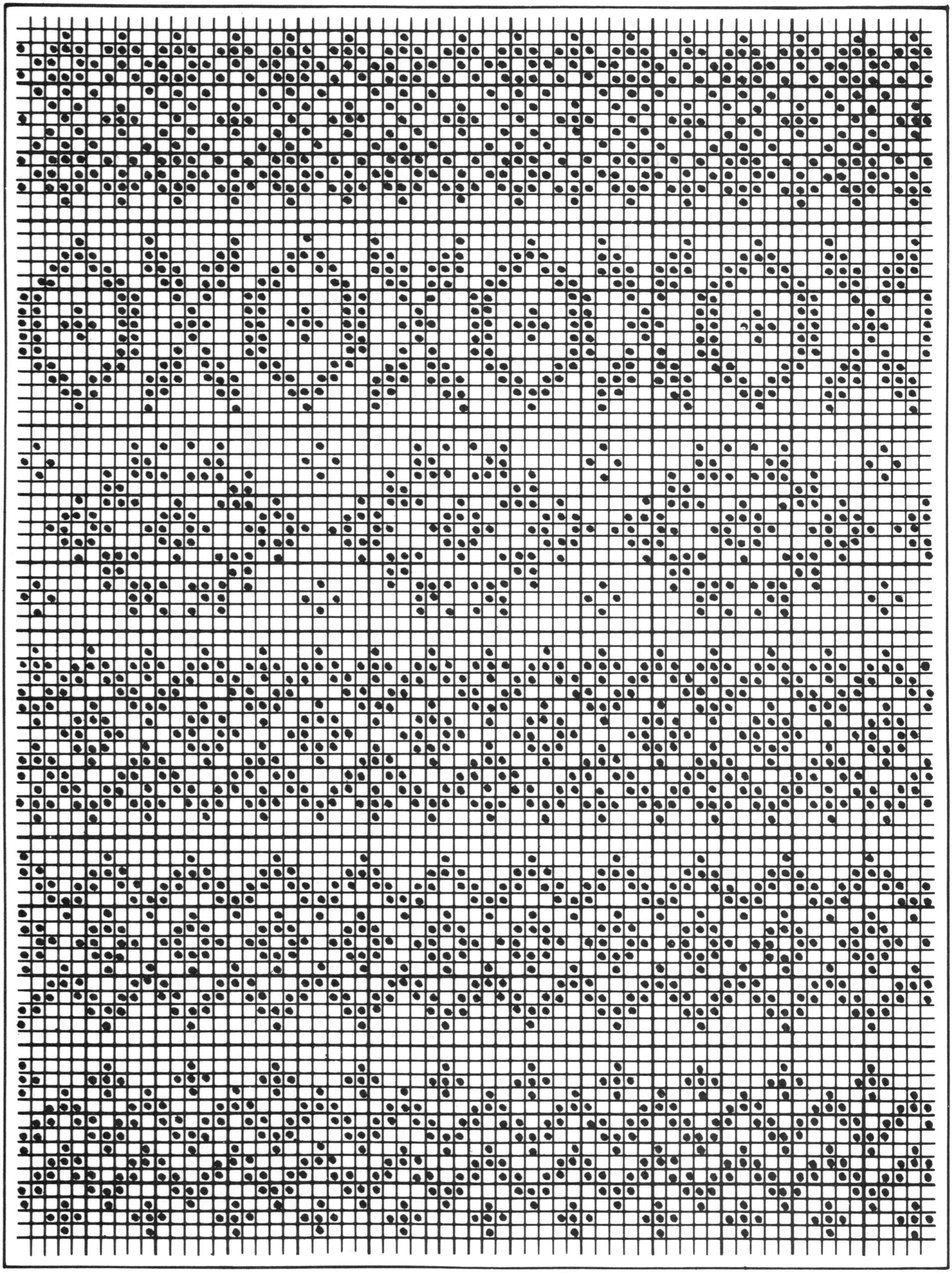

(13)

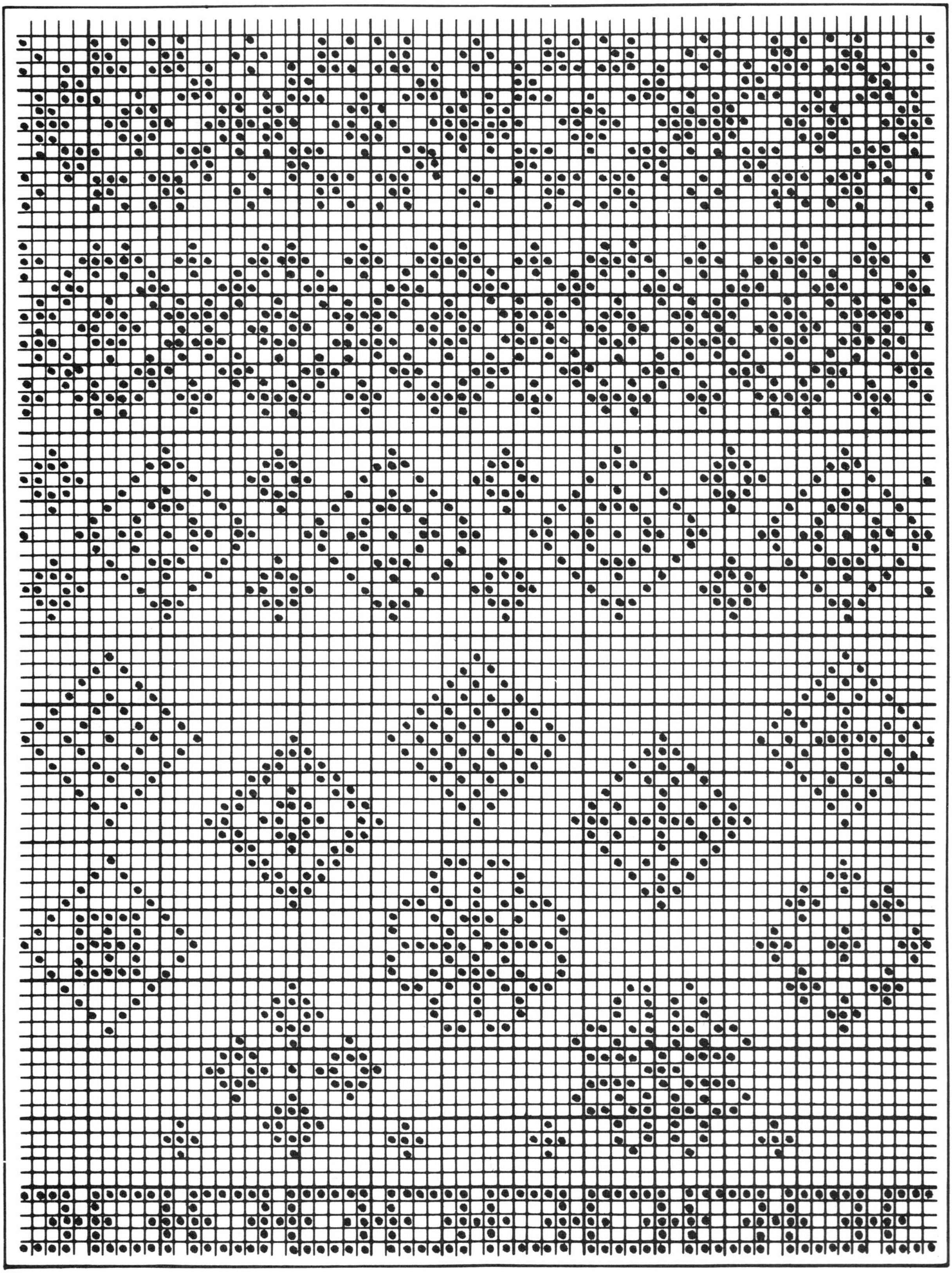

(13)

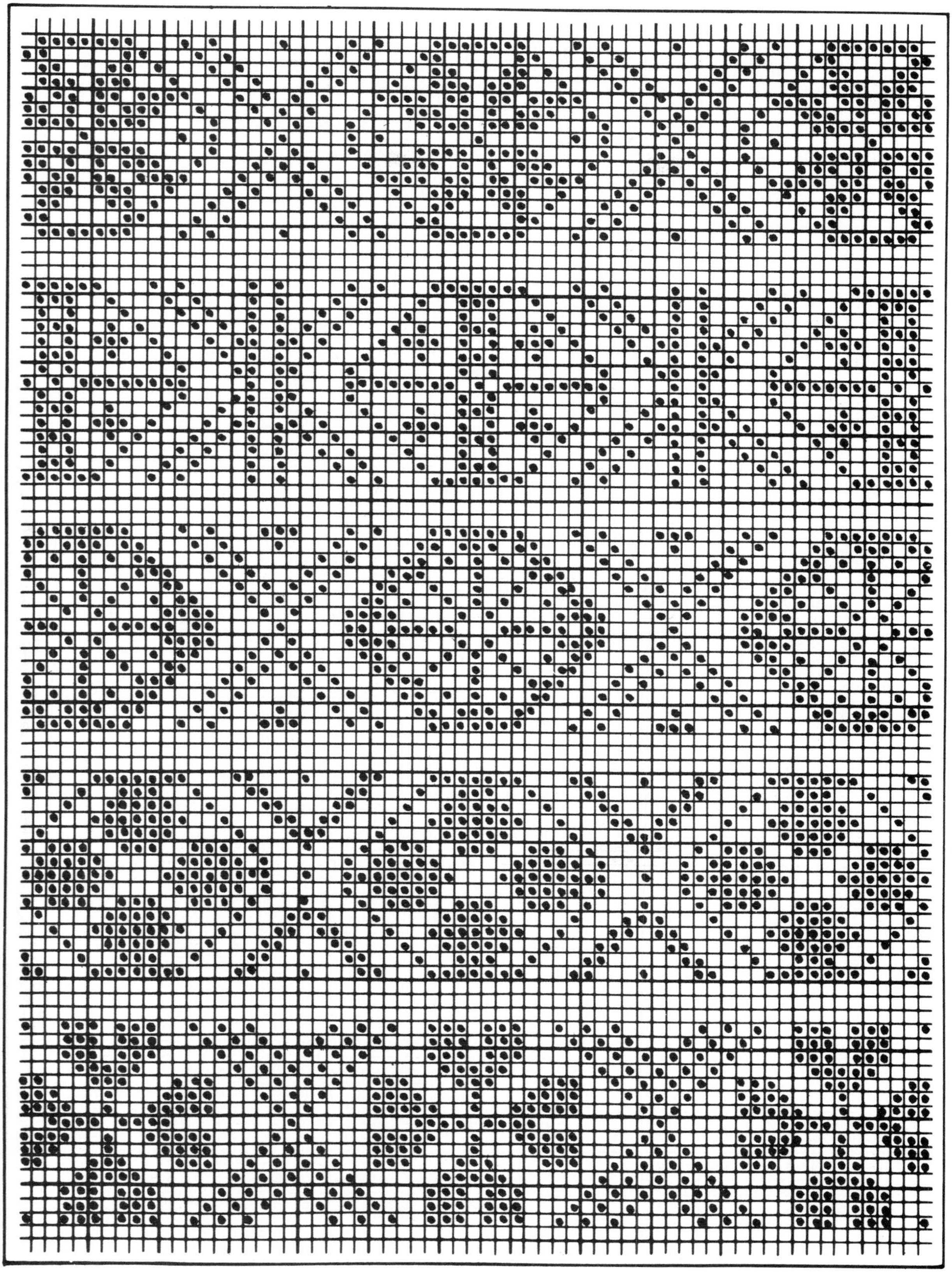

(15)

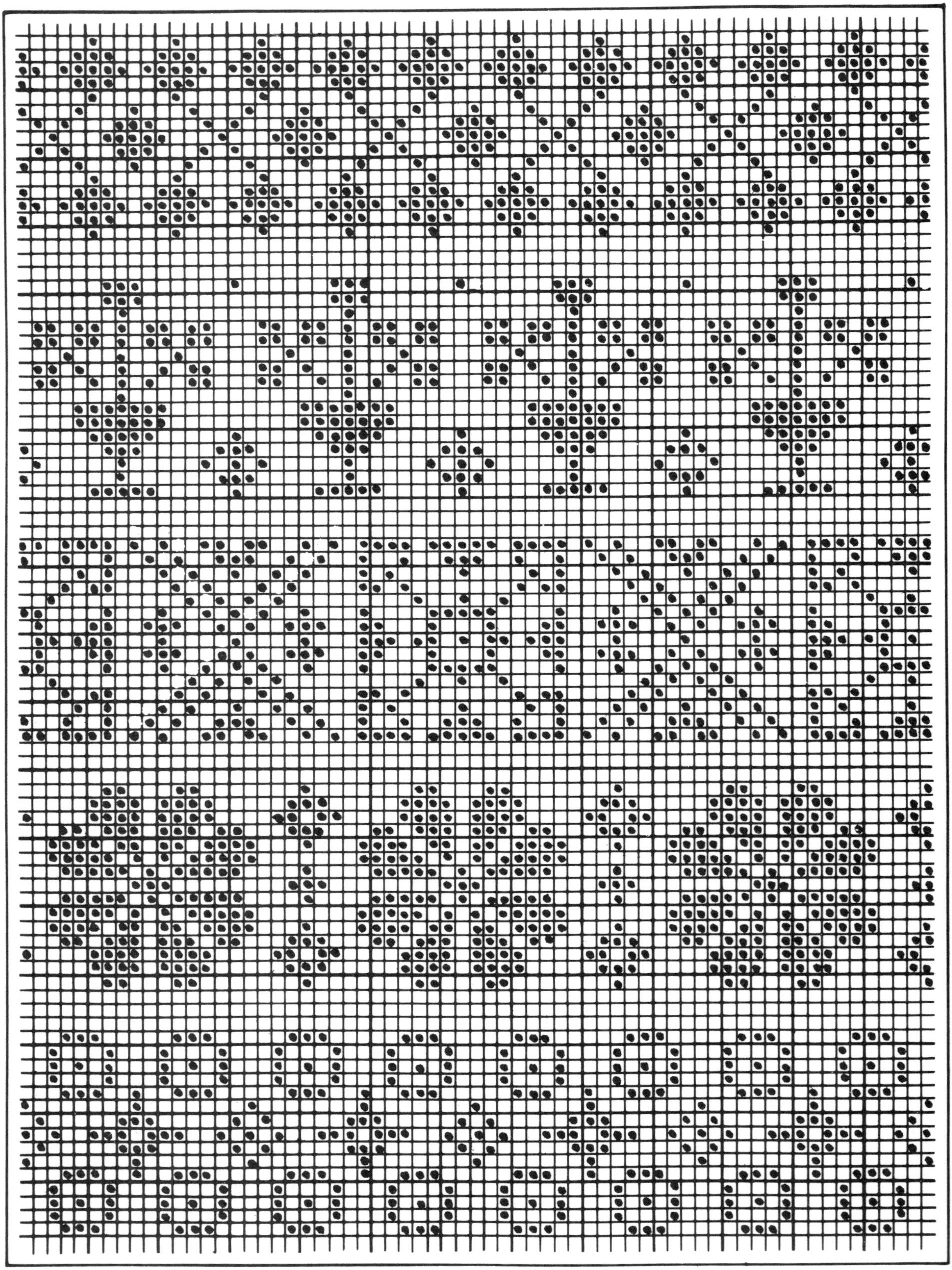

(15)

(15, 16)

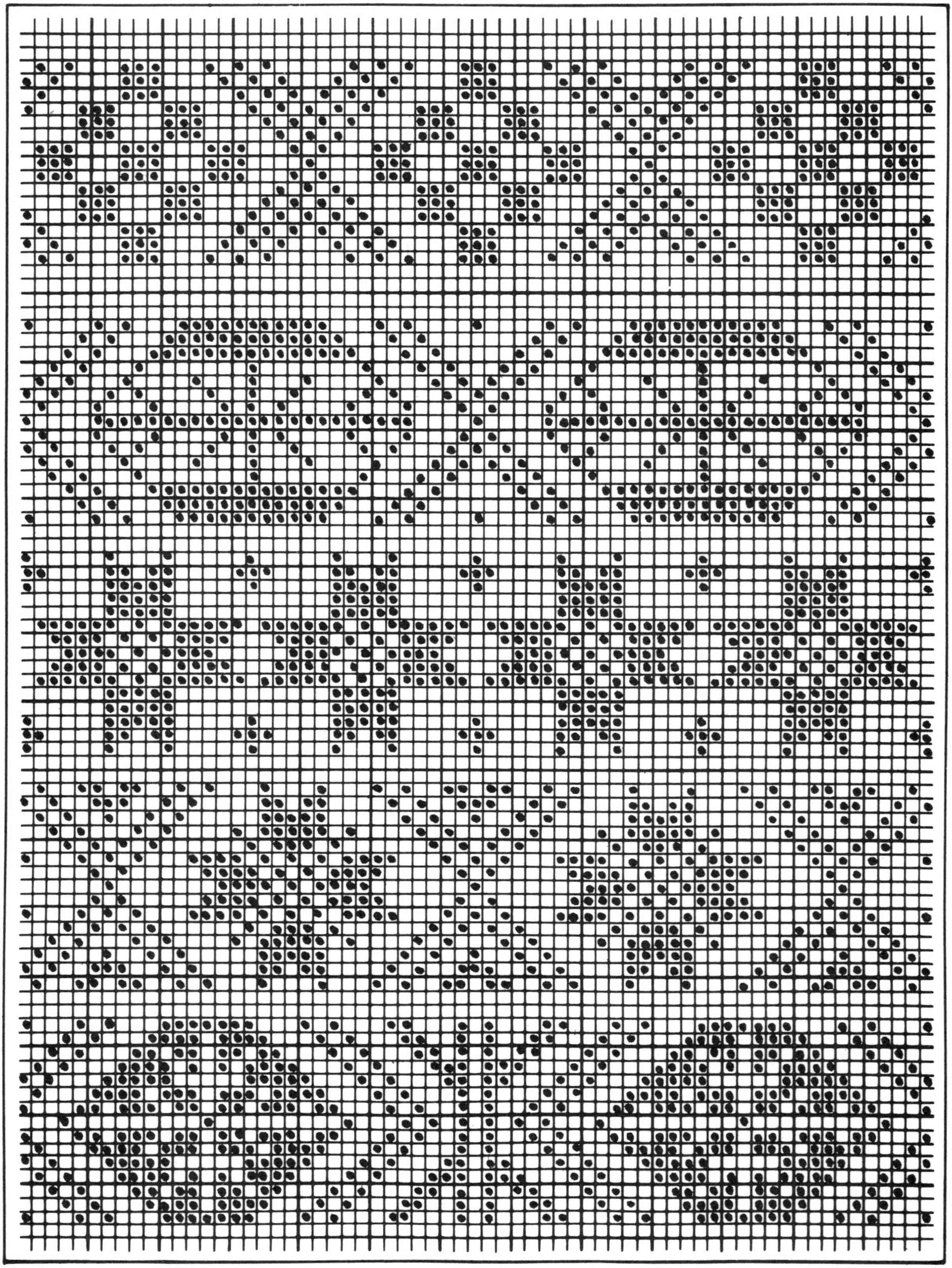

(15)

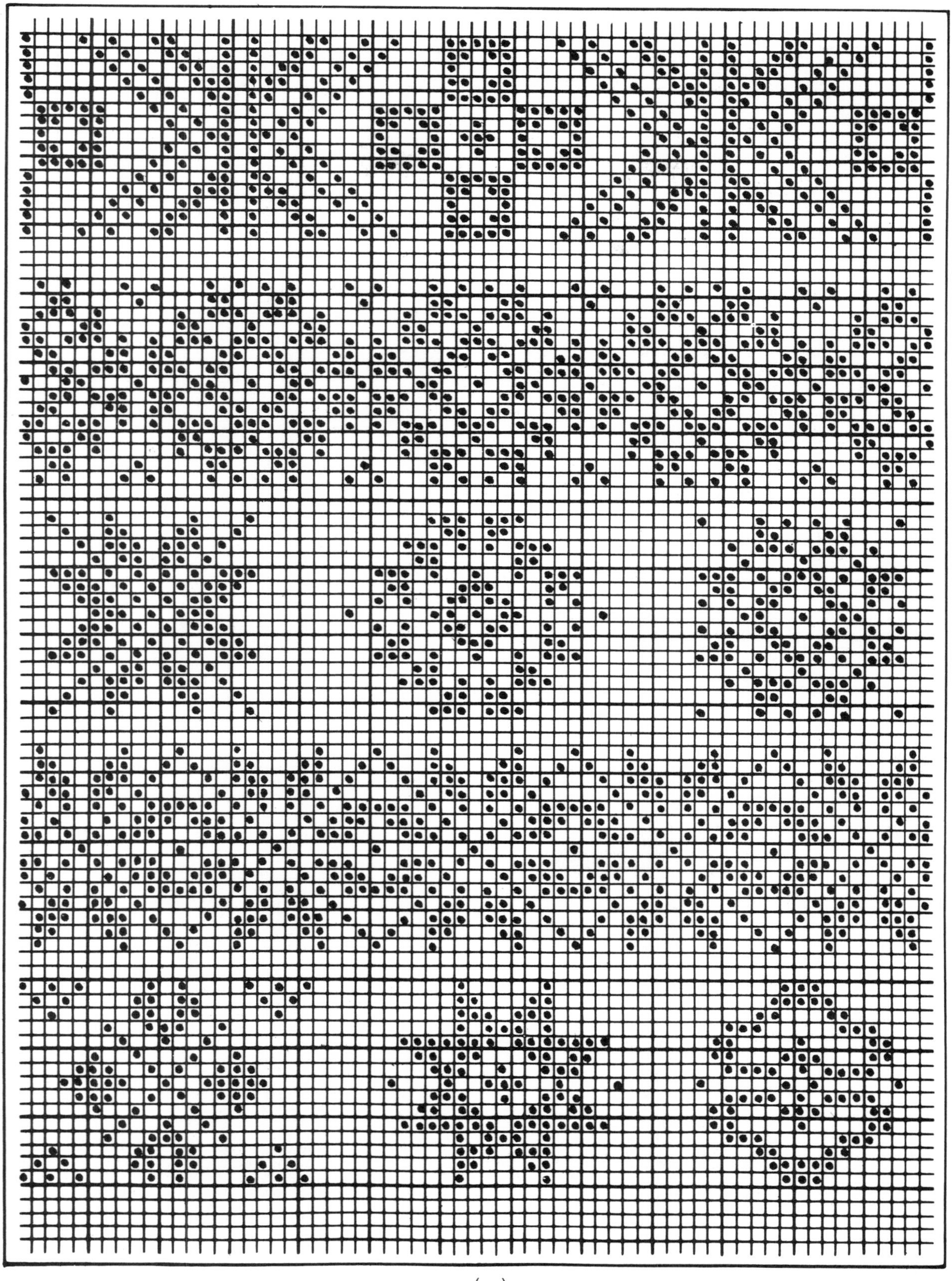

(15)

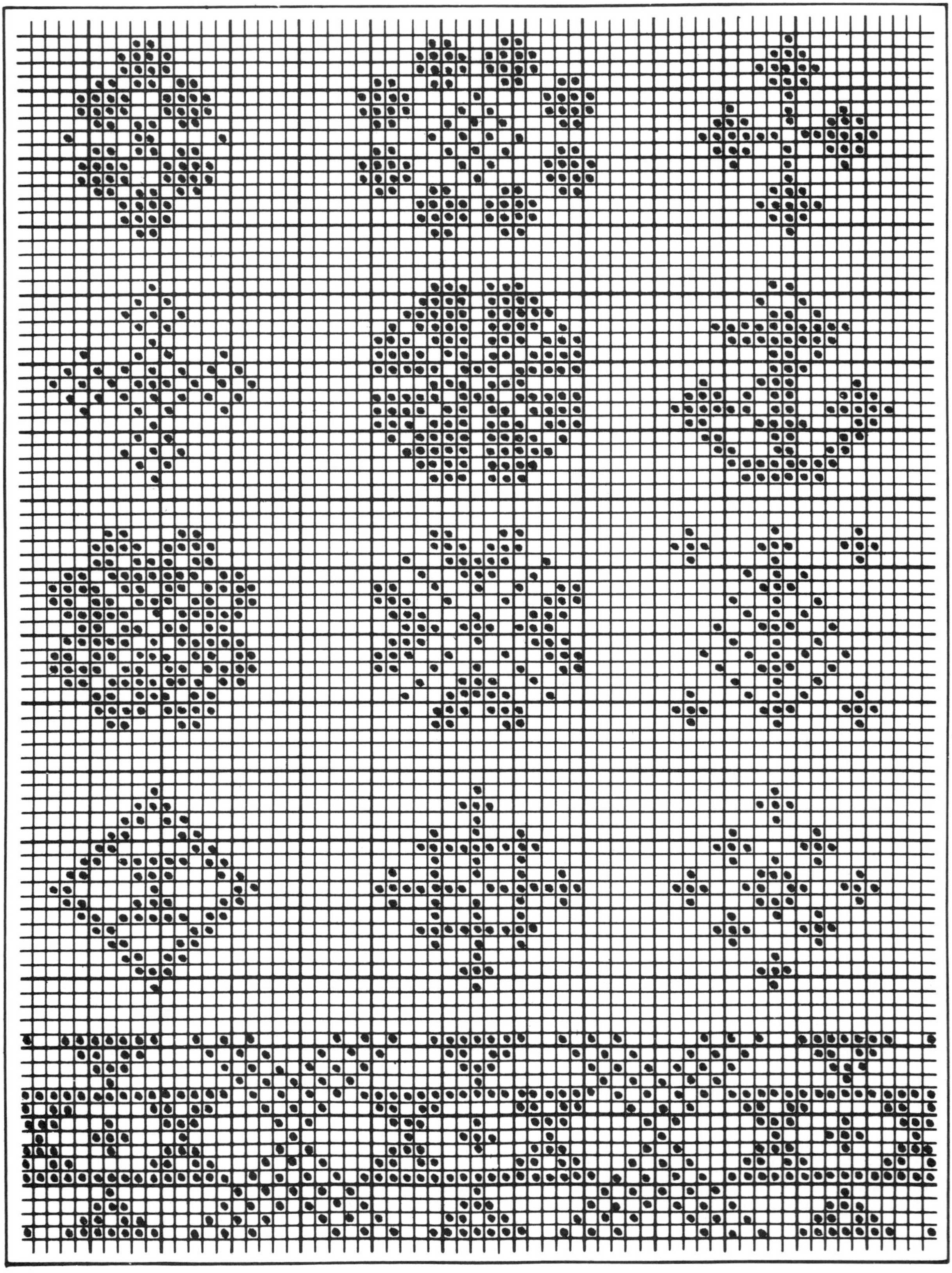

(15)

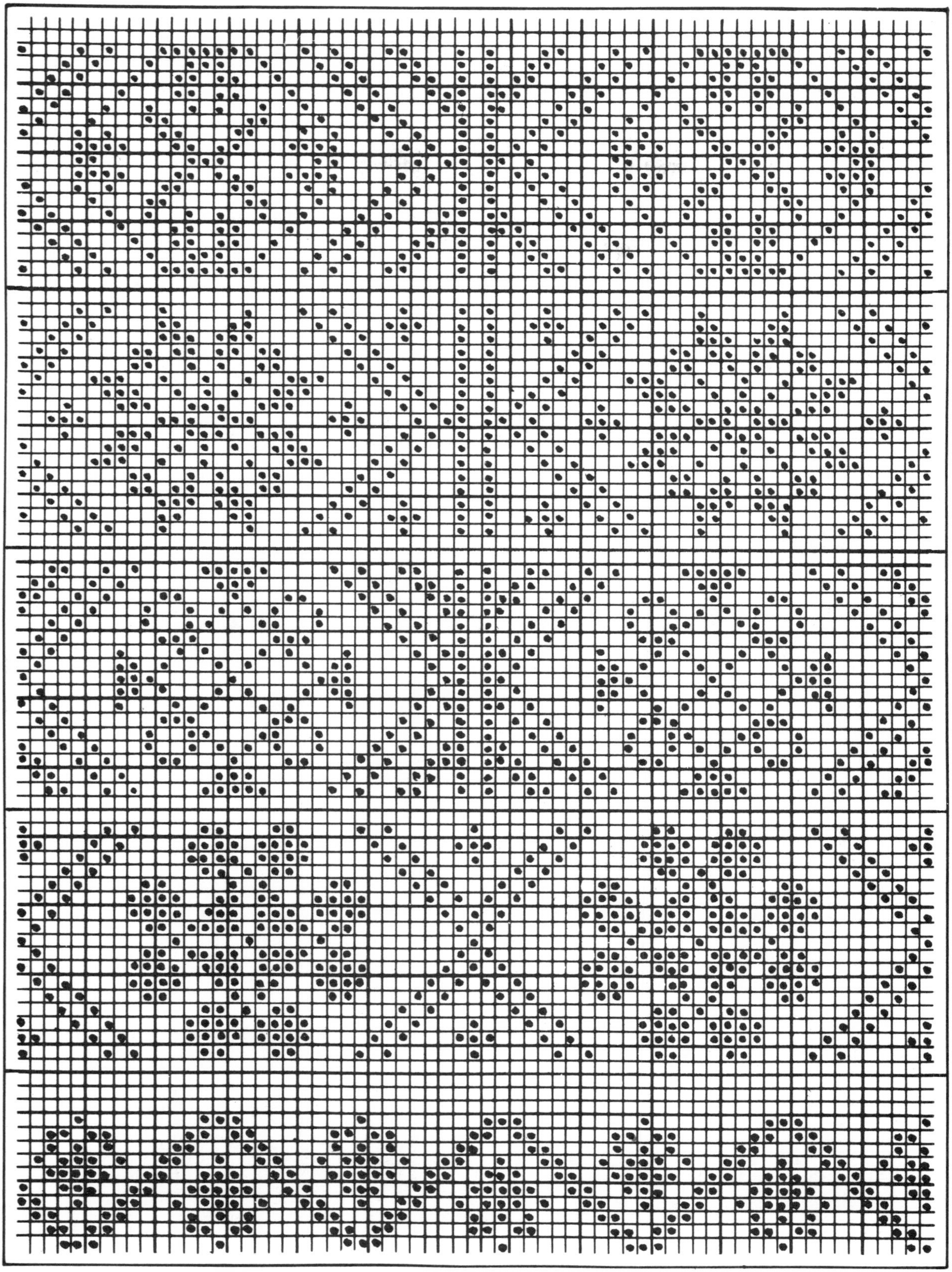

(17)

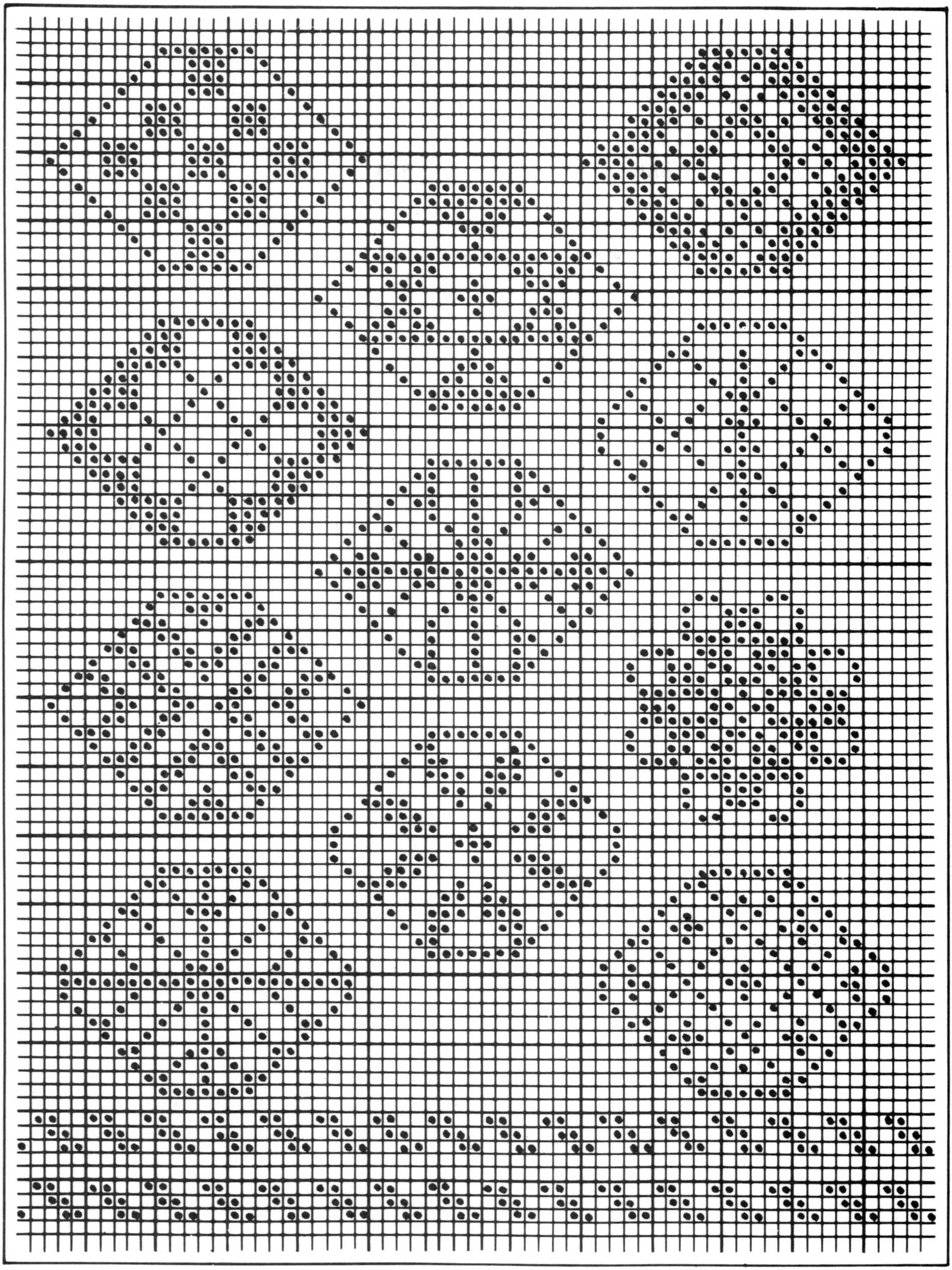

(17)

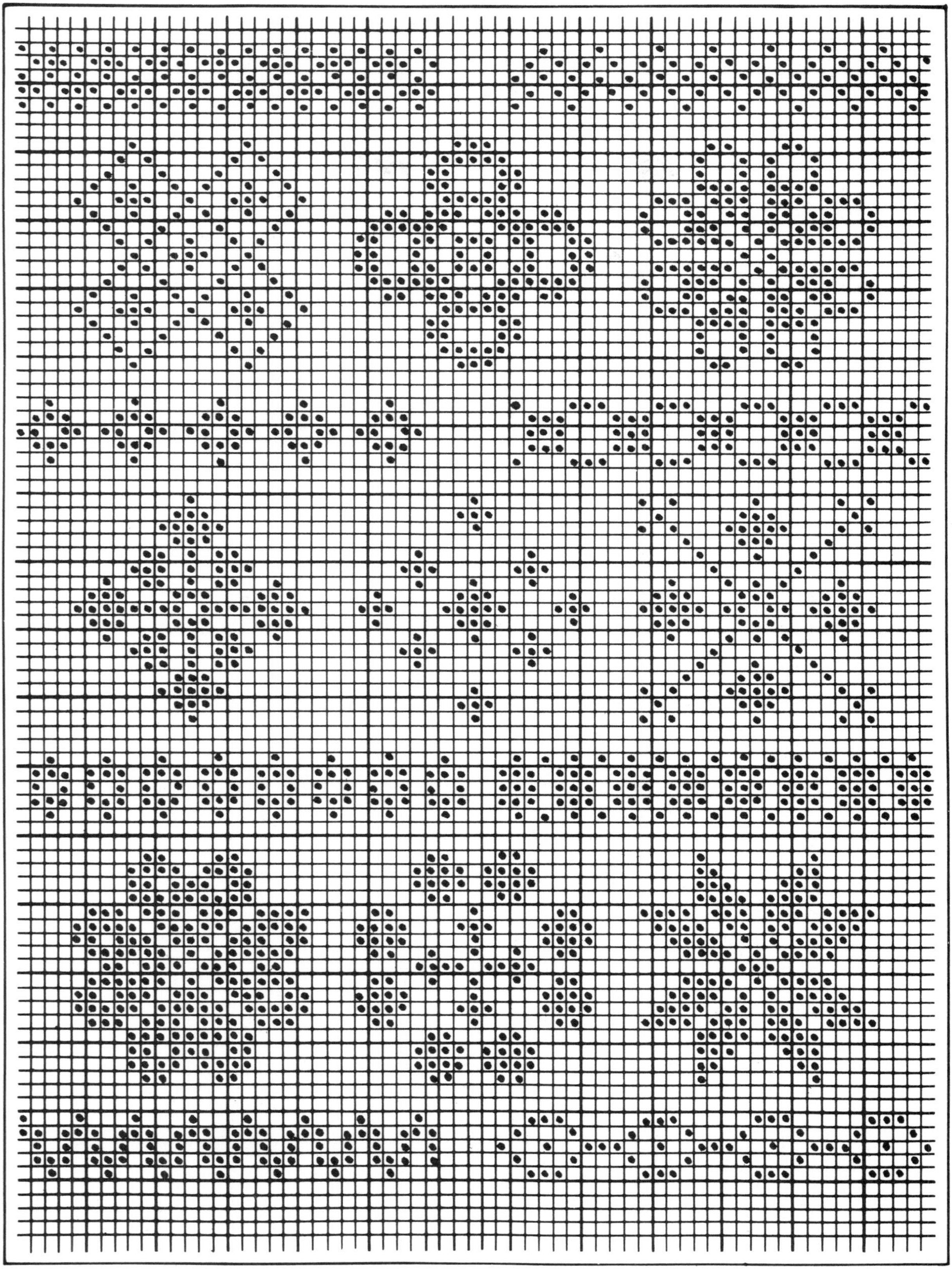

(11, 17)

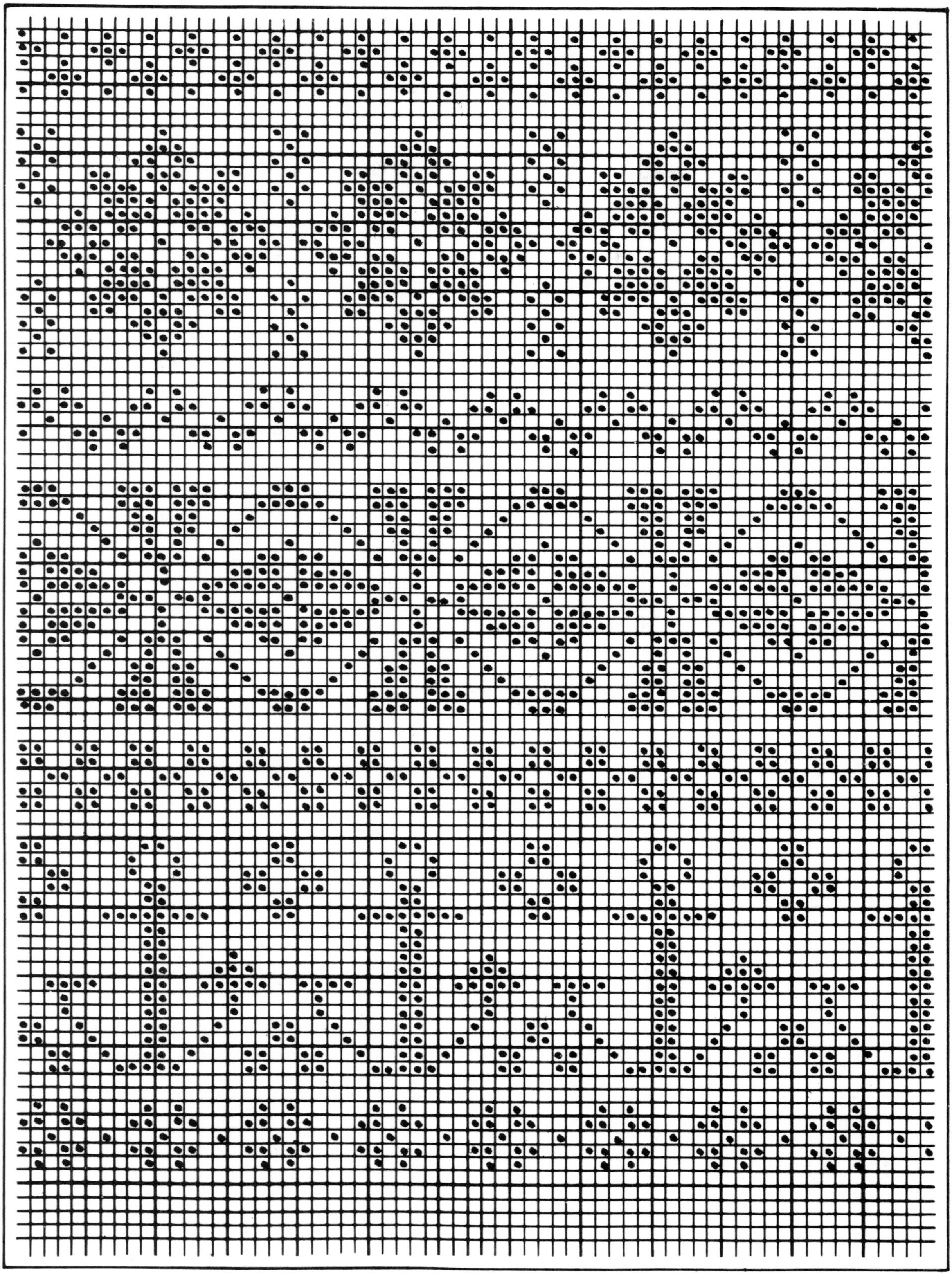

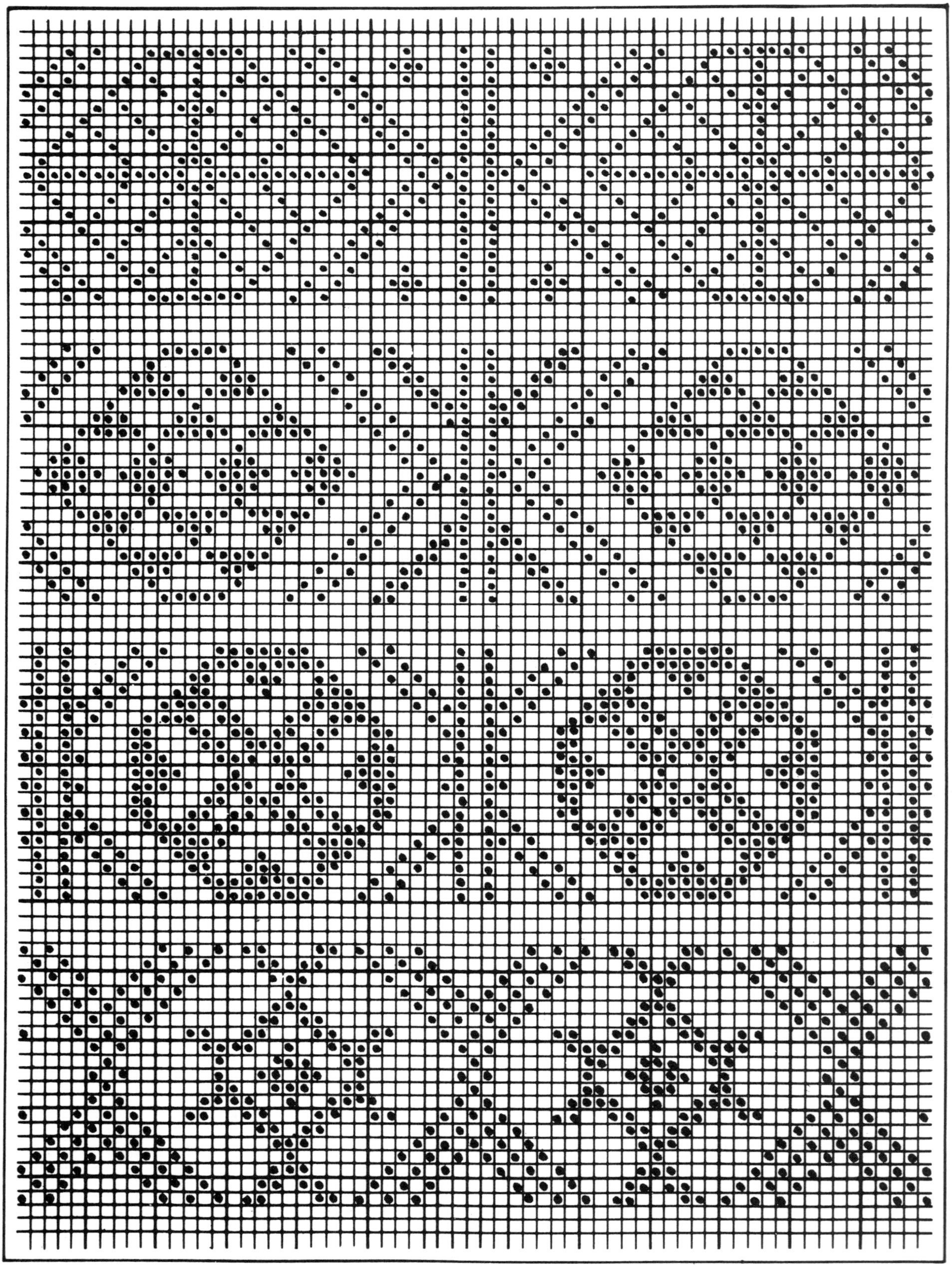

(19)

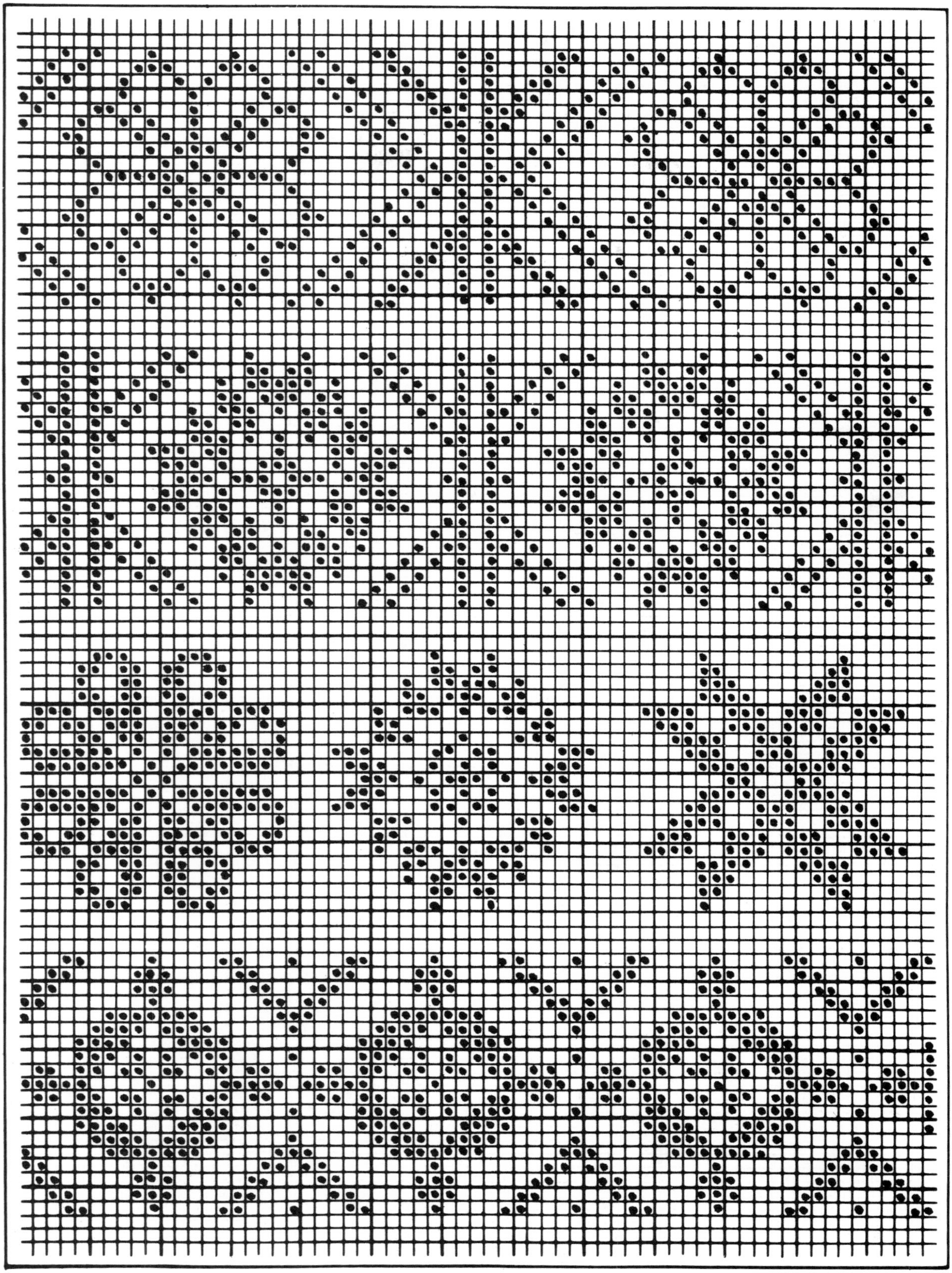

(19)

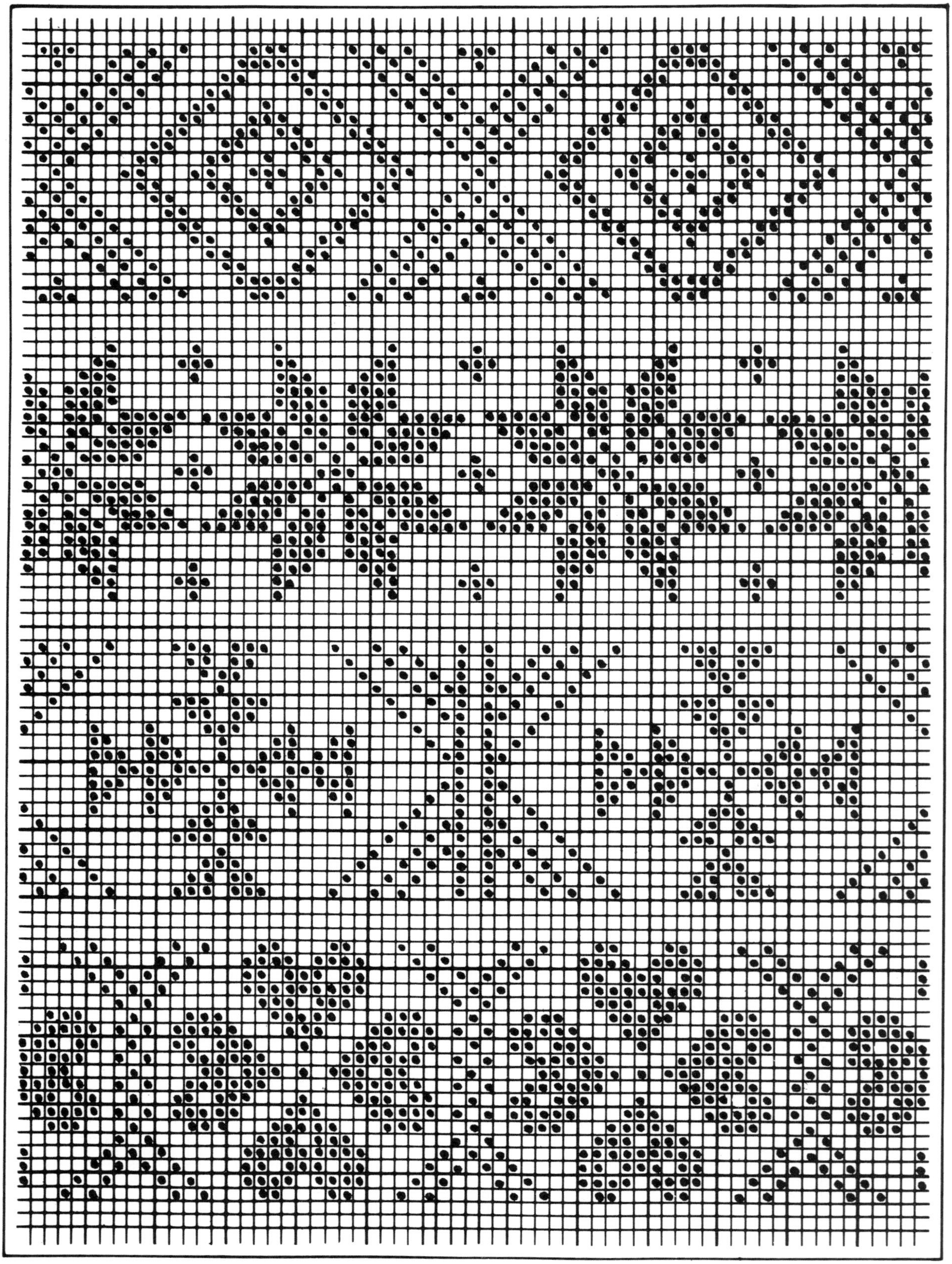

(19)

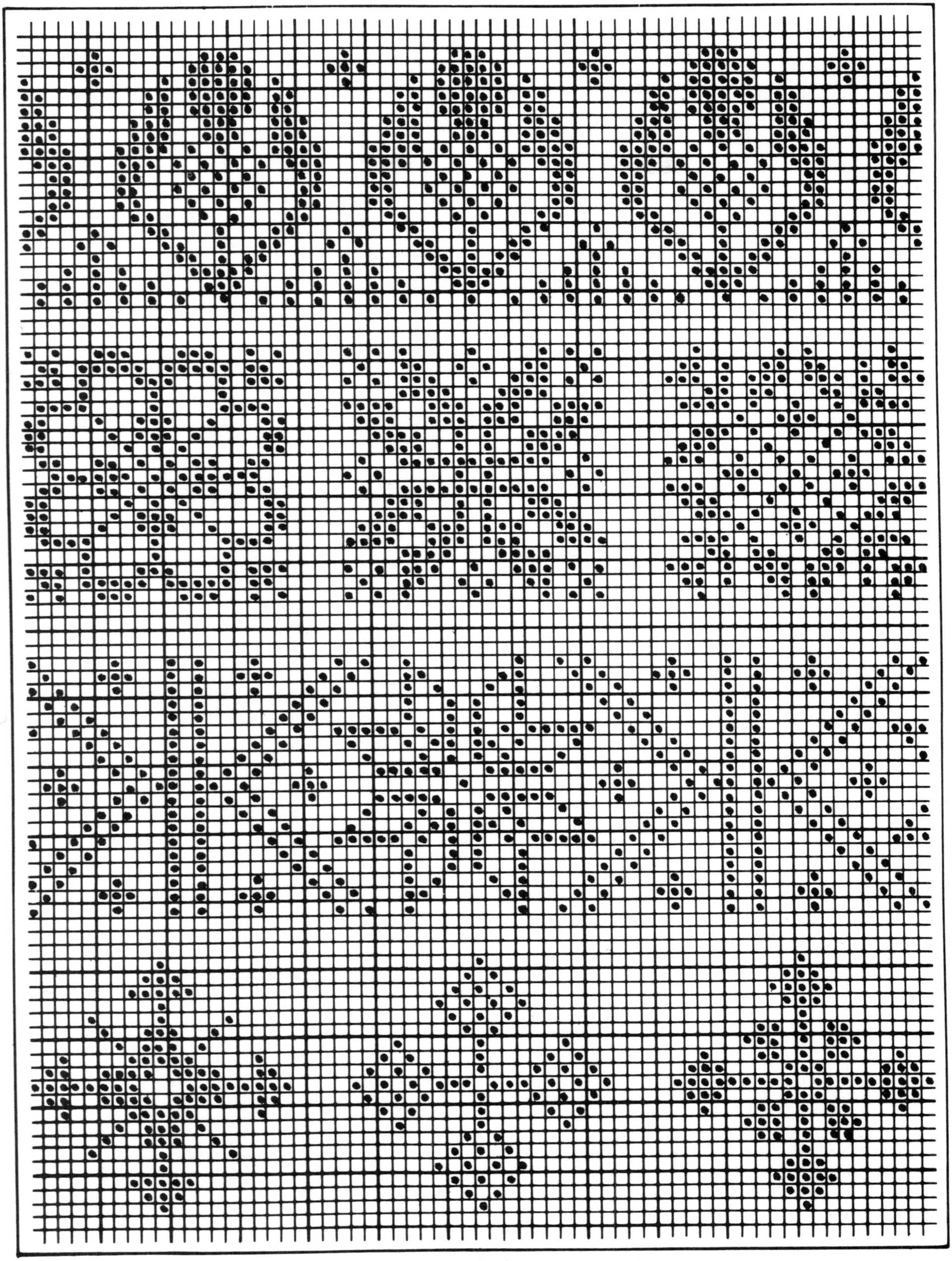

(19)

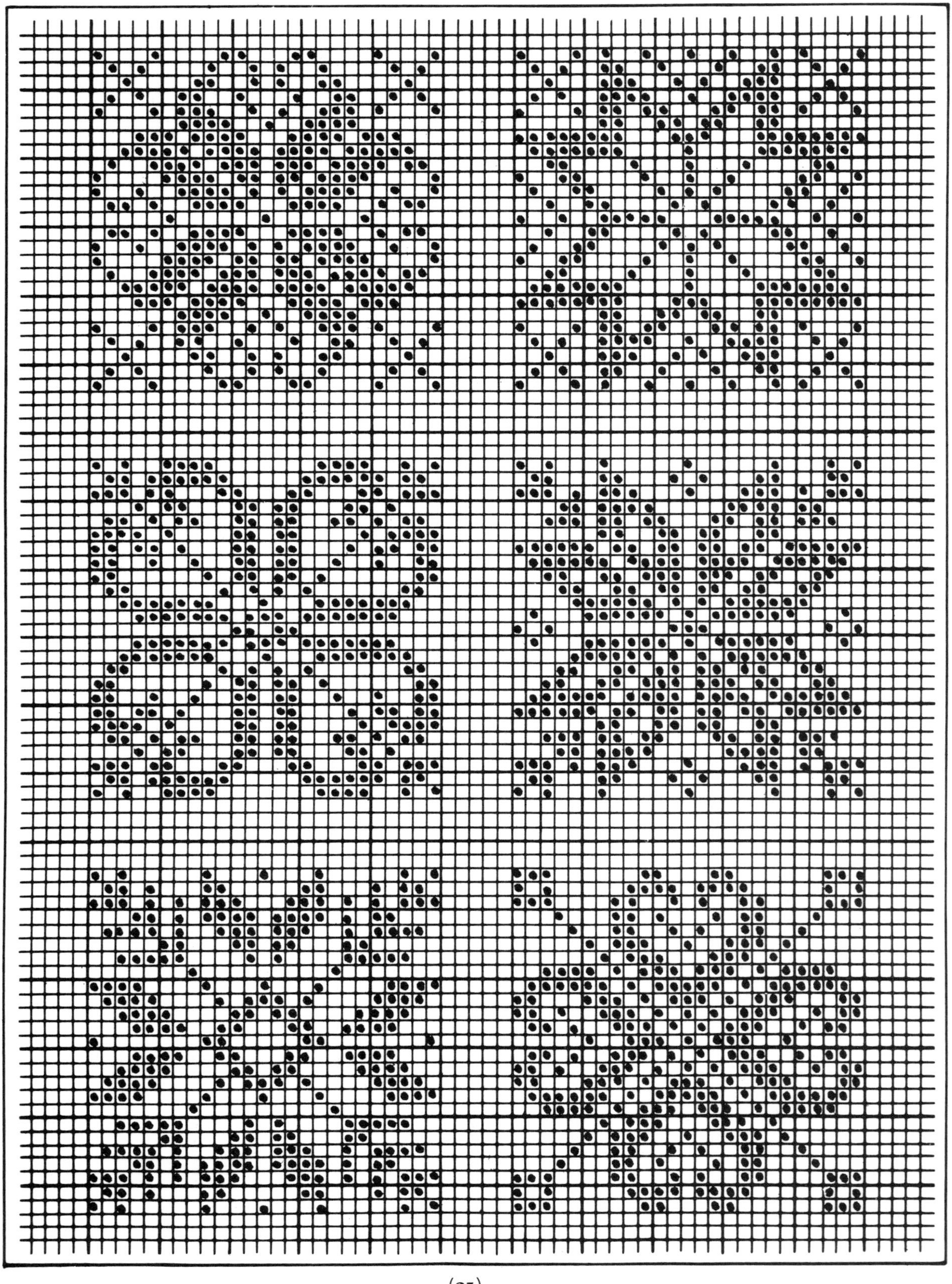

(25)

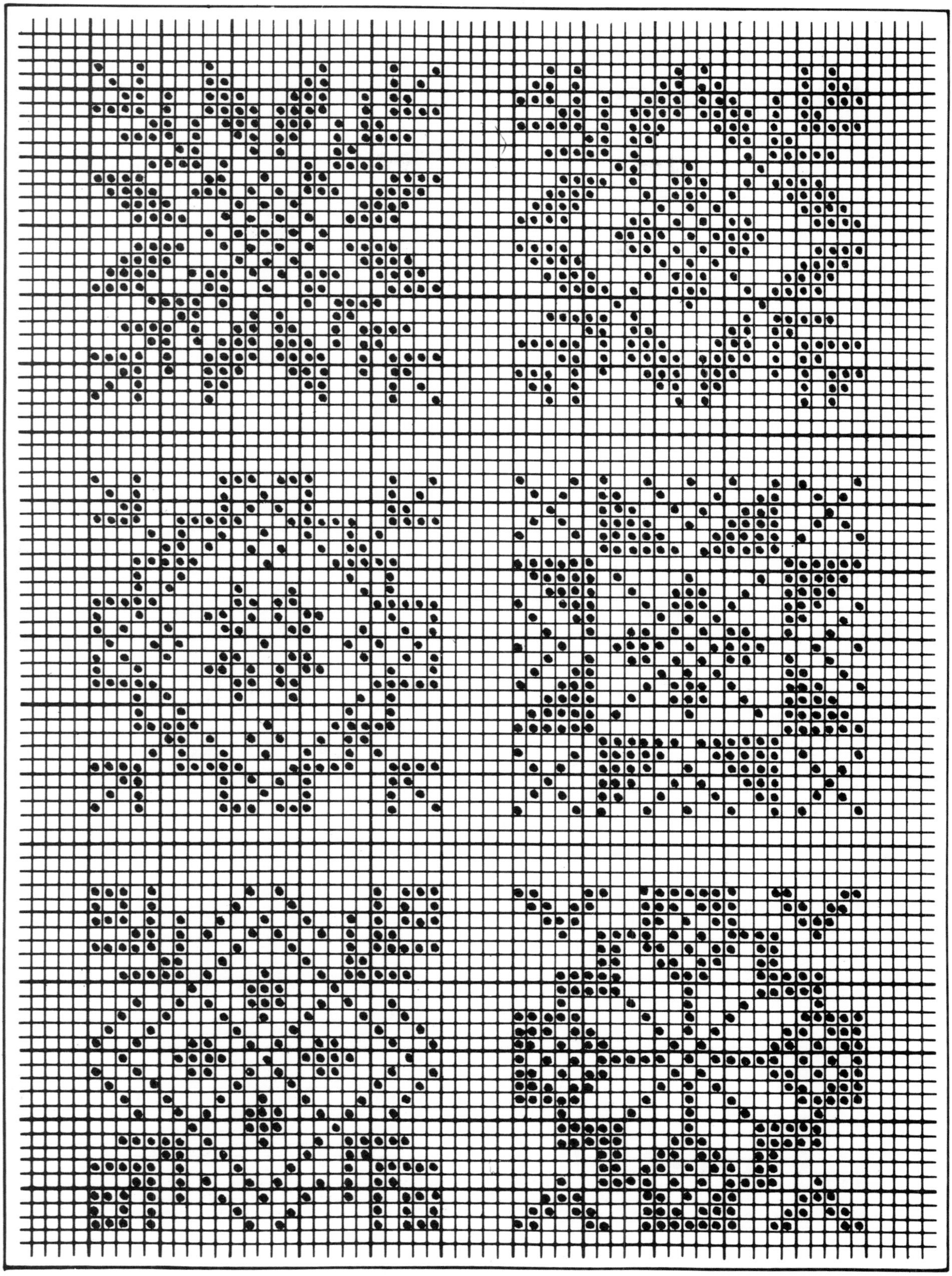

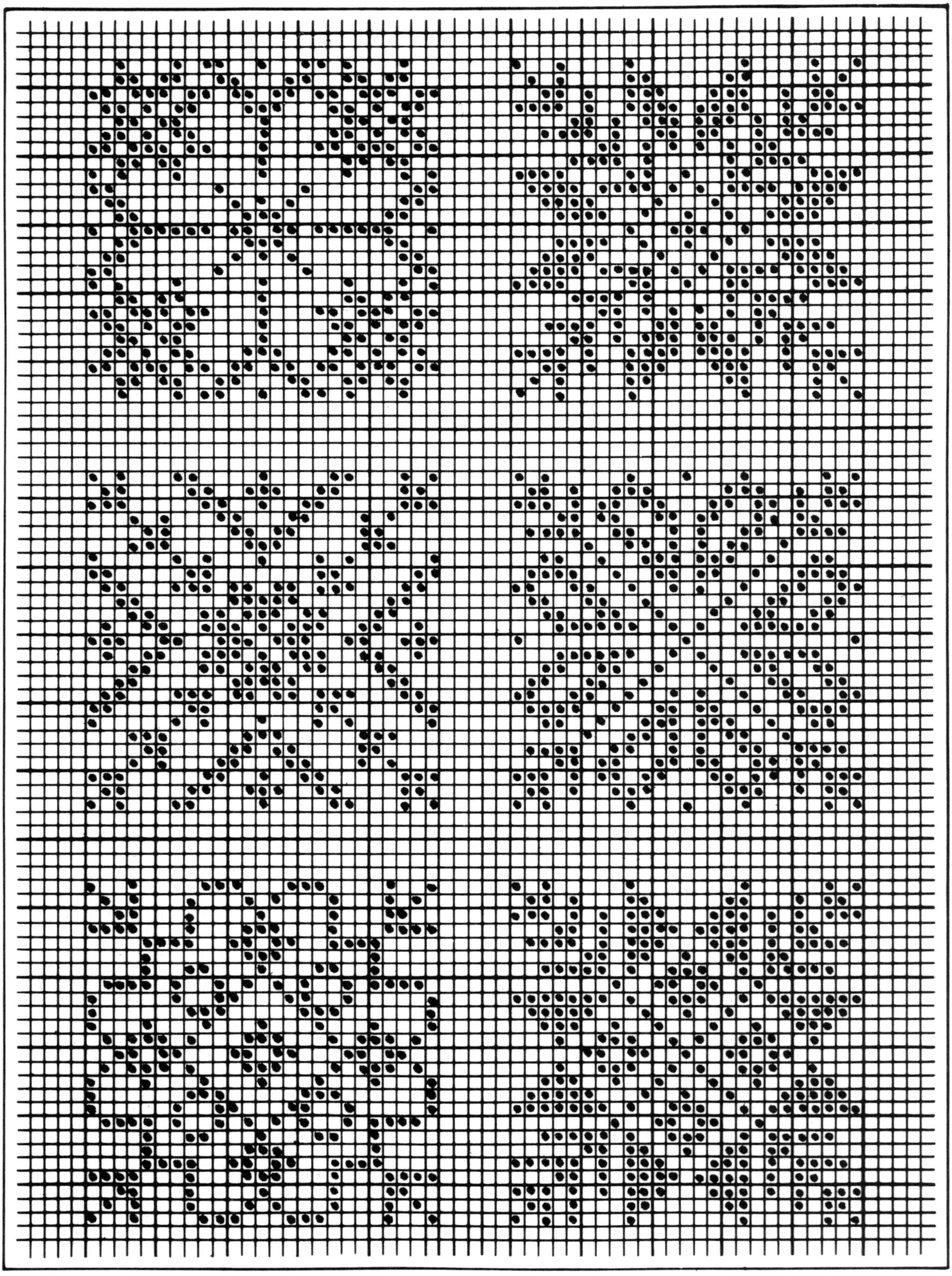

(25, 27)

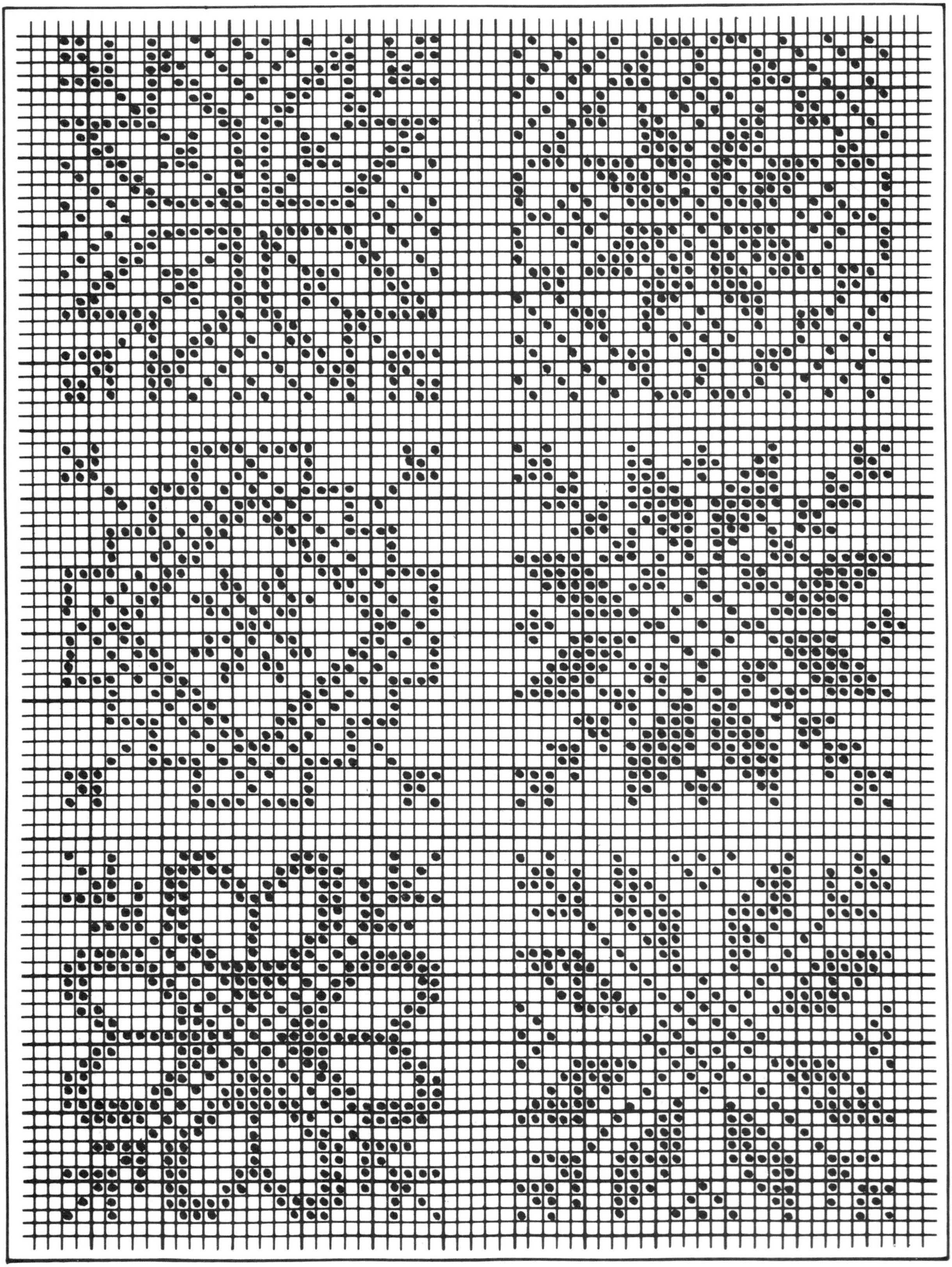

(27)

(19, 31)

124

(19, 31)

(S)

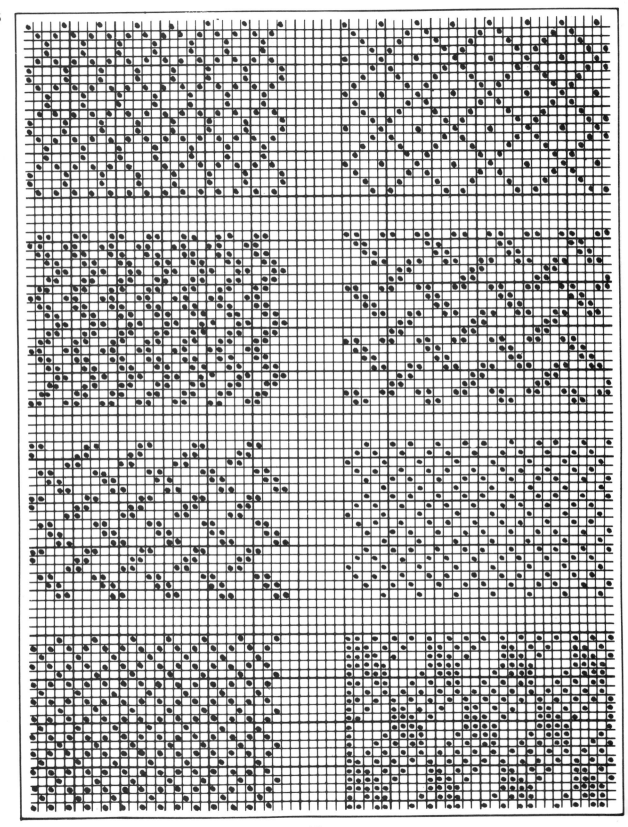

(S)

(AO)

(AO)

(AO)

(AO)

(AO)

(AO)

(AO)

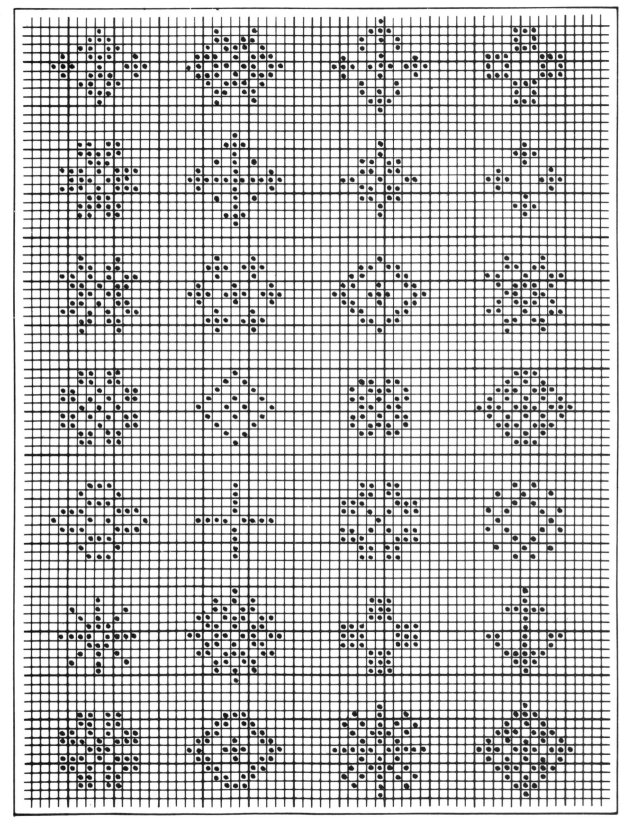

(AO)

(AO)

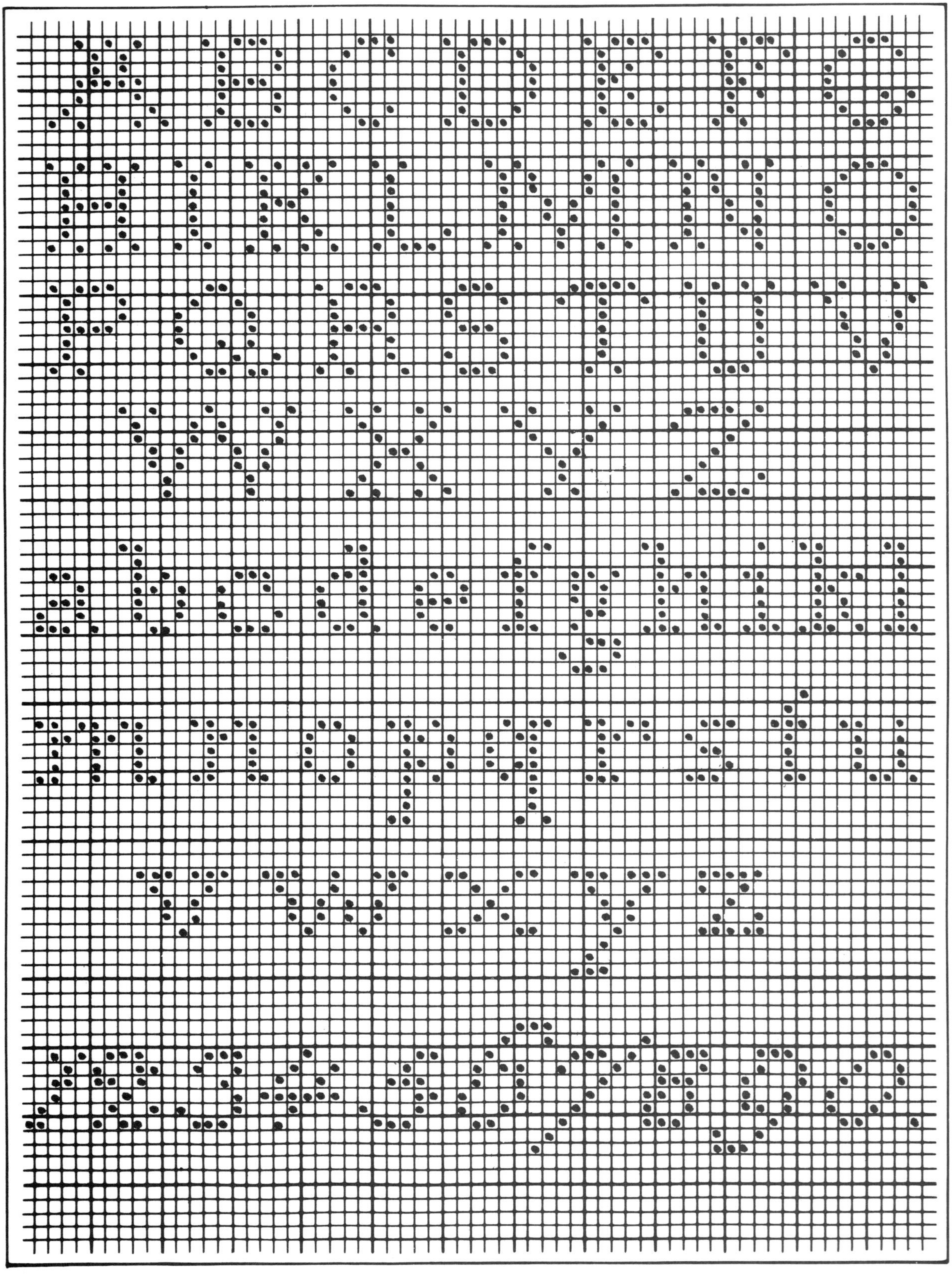

Stockists

Shetland Wool

Jamieson & Smith
(Shetland Wool Brokers) Limited
90 North Road, Lerwick
Shetland Isles
This firm buy wool from Shetland producers and
send it for spinning and dyeing to T. M. Hunter
of Brora, who supply all the wool sold by Jamieson
& Smith. They sell 1 and 2-ply lace weight; 2-ply
jumper weight; 2-ply Soft Spun (chunky); 3-ply
jumper weight (comparable to double knitting);
3-ply Embo (slightly heavier; made from the
rougher part of the fleece). The 2-ply jumper wool
is made up in hanks of approximately 28g (1oz)
which equals 137·16 metres (150 yards). They can
also supply pure Shetland raw wool for spinning
at a 1980 price of £1·70 per kilo, postage to be
added. This can be supplied in natural white,
moorit, grey and black.

T. M. Hunter Limited
Sutherland Wool Mills
Brora, Scotland
Founded in 1901 and involved since the start with
the Shetland knitting industry. Wool on their
cream-coloured shade card (sent on request) is
always in stock. Their second range of fashion
colours changes slightly every year.

Other Yarns, Needles, etc.

Kilbirnie Wools (Scotland) Limited
Station Road
Law
Lanarkshire, Scotland
Can supply a wide range of natural and synthetic
yarns, and any circular or other needles required.
Circular needles are from 40 to 100cm (16 to 42in)
in length.

Circular Needles

Henry Milward & Sons
Studley
Warwickshire, England
and
Abel Morral Limited
Clive Works
Redditch, England

Knitting Belts

Goodlad & Goodlad
The Esplanade
Lerwick, Shetland
Make and supply knitting belts in traditional style
(as shown in this book). They point out that these
are sometimes found very useful by handicapped
knitters. 1980 price is £2·50. Postage is to be added for a weight of 120g (4oz).

Knitting Booklets

Woolcraft
Consumer Liaison Department
Patons & Baldwins Limited
Kilncraigs
Alloa, Scotland
Gives good, traditional instructions for many basic
articles. The 20th edition is now available (1980)
at 50p plus 21p for postage.

Shetland Knitwear

The Shetland Trader
Candlemaker Row
Edinburgh, Scotland
and
Westerhouse
Cunningsburgh
Shetland Islands
Specialists in Fair Isle knitting and lace knitting

The Shetland Woollen Specialists
37 Hanover Street
Edinburgh
Specialists in Fair Isle knitting, lace knitting,
woven rugs, etc.

Knitting Needle Sizes

American	British	Continental (mm)
	7	
6		
	8	4·0
5		
	9	
4		3·5
	10	
3		3·0
	11	
2		
	12	
		2·5
1	13	
0	14	2·0

Exact needle size is not of crucial importance as tension (see p. 56) must always be established. It can, however, be useful to have a variety of needle sizes, and some idea of useful alternatives is given above. Various gadgets exist for measuring needle size.

Bibliography

General Background – Shetland and Fair Isle

Donaldson, Gordon, *Shetland Life Under Earl Patrick*, Oliver & Boyd, Edinburgh, 1958

Edmondston, Eliza, *Sketches and Tales of the Shetland Islands*, Sutherland and Knox, Edinburgh, 1856

Fenton, Alexander, *The Northern Isles: Orkney and Shetland*, John Donald, Edinburgh, 1978

Hamilton, John R. C., *Excavations at Jarlshof, Shetland*, Ministry of Works Archaeological Reports No. 1, London, 1956

Hibbert, Samuel, *A Description of the Shetland Islands*, Edinburgh, 1822, reprinted by T. & J. Manson, Lerwick, 1931

Jakobsen, Jakob, *The Dialect and Place Names of Shetland*, T. & J. Manson, Lerwick, 1897

Linklater, Eric, *Orkney and Shetland*, Robert Hale, London, 1965

Martin, Martin, *A Description of the Western Islands of Scotland circa 1695, to which is added, a Brief Description of the Isles of Orkney and Schetland*, London, 1703

Monteith, Robert, of Eglisha and Gairsa, *The Description of the Isles of Orkney and Zetland*, Sir Robert Sibbald, Geographer Royal for Scotland, Edinburgh, 1711

Morrison, Ian, *The North Sea Earls*, Gentry Books, London, 1973

Nicolson, James R., *Traditional Life in Shetland*, Robert Hale, London, 1978

Russell, Rev. John, *Three Years in Shetland*, Alexander Gardner, Paisley, 1887

Venables, Ursula, *Life in Shetland*, Oliver & Boyd, Edinburgh, 1956
— *Tempestuous Eden*, Museum Press, London, 1952

Williamson, Kenneth, *Fair Isle and its Birds*, Oliver & Boyd, Edinburgh, 1965

Knitting history

Don, Sarah, *Fair Isle Knitting*, Mills & Boon, London, 1979

Grass, Milton & Anna, *Stockings for a Queen*, Heinemann, London, 1967

Hartley, Marie and Ingilby, Joan, *The Old Hand-Knitters of the Dales*, Dalesman Press, Lancaster, 1951, reprinted 1969

Textile History (Editor, K. G. Ponting): numerous articles

Origins of patterns

Ashton, Sir Arthur L. B. (Leigh), *Samplers*, The Medici Society, London, 1926

Bøhn, A. S., *Norwegian Knitting*, Oslo, 1952

Caulfield, Sophia F. A. and Saward, Blanche, *A Dictionary of Needlework*, 1882 (Facsimile Edition, Hamlyn, London, 1972)

Colby, Averil, *Samplers, Yesterday and Today*, B. T. Batsford, London, 1964

Debes, Hans M., *Føroysk Bindingasmynstur*, Thorshaven, 1969

Eesti Riiklik Kirjastus, *Eesti Rahva-Roivaid*, Tallinn, 1957 (Estonian knitting)

Jamieson, Peter A., *Letters on Shetland*, The Moray Press, Edinburgh, 1949

Krafft, Sophie, *Pictorial Weavings of the Viking Age*, Oslo, 1956

Oelsner, G. H., *A Handbook of Weaves*, Dover Publications, Inc., New York, 1952

Olki, Mary; *Kirjokintaista* (Finnish knitting)

Anon: *Patterns for Samplers* (c. 1855)

Flora

Druce, George Claridge, 'Flora Zetlandica', *Supplement to the report of the Botanical Society and Exchange Club*, 1921

Edmondston, Thomas, 'On the Native Dyes of the Shetland Isles', *Trans. Botanical Society of Edinburgh* Vol. 1, 1841
— *A Flora of Shetland*, George Clark & Son, Aberdeen, 1845

Pritchard, N. M., *Proc. Botanical Society of the British Isles* Vol. 2
— *Fair Isle Bird Observatory Report*, No. 24, 1971

Dyes

Bolton, Eileen M., *Lichens for Vegetable Dyeing*, Studio Books, Longacre Press, London, 1960

Lesch, Alma, *Vegetable Dyeing*, David & Charles, Newton Abbott, 1974

Mairet, Ethel, *A Book on Vegetable Dyes*, 11th edition, Faber & Faber, London, 1952

Thurstan, Violetta, *The Use of Vegetable Dyes for Beginners*, 10th revised edition, Dryad Press, Leicester, 1967

Knitting techniques

Thomas, Mary, *Knitting Book*, Hodder &
Stoughton, London, 1938; Dover edition 1978
— *Book of Knitting Patterns*, Hodder &
Stoughton, London, 1943

Thompson, Gladys, *Patterns for Guernseys and Jerseys*,
2nd edition, B. T. Batsford, London, 1969
Woolcraft, 20th edition, Patons & Baldwins, Alloa,
Scotland, 1980

Index